LITTLE TOWN
blues

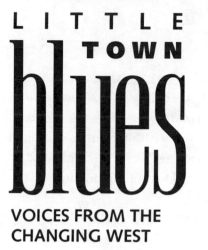

LITTLE TOWN blues

VOICES FROM THE CHANGING WEST

TEXT
RAYE C. RINGHOLZ

PHOTOGRAPHS
K. C. MUSCOLINO

GIBBS·SMITH
➔P
PUBLISHER

PEREGRINE SMITH BOOKS
SALT LAKE CITY

First edition
95 94 93 92   5 4 3 2 1

Text copyright © 1992 by Raye C. Ringholz
Photographs copyright © 1992 by K. C. Muscolino

This is a Peregrine Smith Book, published by
Gibbs Smith, Publisher
P.O. Box 667
Layton, UT 84041

Design by Clarkson Creative
Cover illustration by K. C. Muscolino

Manufactured in the United States of America
Library of Congress Cataloging-in-Publication Data

Ringholz, Raye Carleson.
        Little-town blues : voices from the changing west /
Raye C. Ringholz and K. C. Muscolino.
                p. cm.
        ISBN 0-87905-447-6 (pbk.)
        1. Rural renewal—West (U.S.)—Case studies. 2. Tourist
trade—Social aspects—West (U.S.)—Case studies. 3. West (U.S.)—
Social conditions. I. Muscolino, K. C. II. Title.
HT441.A17R56 1992
307.76'2'0978—dc20   91-40217
                                                      CIP

For Fred and Lucille Carleson

CONTENTS

ACKNOWLEDGEMENTS

It is very difficult to interpret the philosophies and lifestyles of a place without having lived there. I am therefore doubly grateful to the residents of small towns/resorts depicted in this book for their willingness to share their views and inform me about their towns. The friendliness and hospitality I have experienced in researching this work are tangible indications that the spirit of the Old West may be changed, but it is not lost.

My thanks to our good Moab, Utah, friends Mitch and Mary Williams, Ken and Jane Sleight, Pete Plastow, and Sam and Adrienne Taylor. I appreciate the information and time given by Lin Ottinger, Tom Arnold, Ralph Miller, Merv Lawton, Mayor Tom Stocks, Hans Weibel, Dave Bierschied, Bette Stanton, Tom Shellenberger, Jimmy Walker, John Groo, Bill Groff, Carl Rappe, Russ Van Koch, Tex McClatchy, Lloyd Pierson, Superintendent Harvey Wickware, Bob Jones, Don Knowles, and John and Marilyn Bicking.

Sedona, Arizona, was opened to me through the help of my long-time friend Dolly Makoff. Thanks to Ray Steele, Earl and Ginny Vanderan, Oma Bird, Bill and Jan Bliss, Mary Lou Keller, Sakina, Sherman and Martha Loy, Marian Herrman, Don Pratt, Frank Miller, Nassan Gobran, and Ranger Ron Plapp for introducing me to this beautiful place.

There were many who helped me know the "New West" of Jackson Hole, Wyoming. My appreciation to my life-long friends Bob and Claire McConaughy, to Bill and Story Resor, Earl Hardeman, Virginia Huidekoper, Jack Huyler, Cliff Hansen, Mickey Waller, Frannie Huff, and Len Carlman. John Bradley, Robert Coapman, Gene and Nancy Hoffman, Paul Walton, Bland Hoke, Ralph Gill, Paul McCollister, Dave Spackman, Dick Albrecht, Kelly and Shelley Rubrecht, and Parthenia Stinnett were others who shared their time and insight.

I am grateful to former Mayor Bill Stirling, Carol O'Dowd, Sepp and Janie Kessler, and Fritz Benedict of Aspen, Colorado; Art Goodtimes, Rick Silverman, Johnnie Stevens, George Greenbank, Virginia Eggar, Gary Hickcox, and Pamela Lifton-Zoline of Telluride, Colorado; Bob Mathis, Miles Rademan, Vickie Shephard, Gary Weiss, Tom Clyde, Sally Elliott, Lloyd Evans, and Chief Frank Bell of Park City, Utah; Dr. Bruce Godfrey, Utah State University, Logan, Utah; and Dr. Thayne Robson, Bureau of Business and Economic Research, University of Utah, Salt Lake City, Utah.

My friends Leon and Barbara Watson gave me insight into St. George, Utah; Gus Cordova, Don Laine and John Holland introduced me to Taos, New Mexico; and Mike Patelle, Suzanne Hubner, and Debbie Jaramillo talked with me about Santa Fe, New Mexico. Homer Fancher, of Bullhead City, Arizona; Mike Whitfield, Driggs, Idaho; Ward Roylance, Torrey, Utah; and Terry Minger, of Robert Redford's Center for Resource Management, Denver, Colorado, were most helpful.

There are many others in the libraries and museums throughout the West whose assistance has been invaluable.

Last, but certainly not least, my deepest appreciation to Gibbs Smith for his help in envisioning and publishing this book. Thanks, too, to Madge Baird and Steve Chapman of Peregrine Smith Books, and to my able editor Joanna Hurley, whose editorial eye and attention to detail have been indispensable.

Once again I am indebted to my husband, Joe, who was a valued traveling companion and a ready sounding-board.

K. C. Muscolino's photographs are outstanding and my collaboration with her has been a true delight.

PHOTOGRAPHER'S STATEMENT

Working on a project like this gave me an excuse and an opportunity to seriously explore these small western towns. I chose not to focus on the obvious. Most of us know what congested Main Streets look like and have seen that one-too-many curio shop. I wanted to photograph what was behind those false-fronted buildings, to make portraits of those local old-timers who know and have lived the history that created these western towns, as well as the newcomers creating history today. Most of all, I wanted to show the layers of growth which have taken place.

There were many people who generously gave their time, sat patiently for my portraits and shared their stories. I am grateful.

Thanks to Bob Jones at Moab's Tag-a-long Tours, and Lou Centrella at Jackson Hole Llamas for the wonderful excursions.

My family, Joe, Nick and Max, were wonderfully understanding during my pursuit of a photograph.

Gibbs Smith had the confidence in an emerging concept. Madge Baird helped define it.

Raye Ringholz had the perseverance to pursue her love of writing, and I am grateful she included me.

K. C. Muscolino

INTRODUCTION

In creating this book, I hoped to portray a kind of living history of the growth that is changing the American West today—a growth spawned by floundering mining and agricultural economies turning to tourism as a salvation, and manifested in progressive urbanization of once-rural communities and commercialization of the outdoors.

If there's a mountain to hike or ski, redrock backcountry to explore, a waterway to play on, or a desert oasis to green into a golf course, it's being developed by entrepreneurs with hordes of tourists and recreationers hard on their heels. Within a few short years, the immigrants follow and authentic mining camps, rustic cow towns, pioneer farming communities—historic signatures of the American West—succumb to cosmetic changes that leave them little resemblance to their original selves. Even worse, they all start to look alike.

As a lifelong westerner and Park City, Utah, historian for many years, I have witnessed this progression firsthand. I moved to "the Park" over seventeen years ago. Since I was a little girl, I have been charmed by this former mining town tucked in a crease of the Wasatch Mountains.

I can remember the fifties when mining slumped and Main Street held little but boarded-up buildings. Rickety wooden stairs climbed the steep hills to rows of empty, gabled frame houses in the hall-and-parlor, shotgun, and pyramid styles that were typical of boom camps throughout the West.

The sixties and seventies brought new life when the United Park City Mines Company—which had virtually collapsed under depressed metal prices, escalating production costs, and nasty labor disputes—switched emphasis from underground mining to skiing and created the Treasure Mountain Resort (forerunner of the Park City Ski Area).

City boundaries stretched northward with a golf course surrounded by a few condominiums and small neighborhoods of contemporary homes. The ghost revived as gourmet restaurants, go-go parlors with mock Victorian decor, melodrama in the antiquated Egyptian Theatre, and even a nightclub stripper brought the community back into the twentieth century.

But the old landmarks were still in place: the miner's Cozy Bar with its sign reading "First Chance" on one side and "Last Chance" on the other, St. Mary's Catholic Church, the Elks and Masonic halls that survived the "big fire of 1898," City Hall sitting over a territorial dungeon still holding leg irons and barred cells with prisoners' graffiti on the walls, the Motherlode that was short on chic but served the best baconburgers in town.

Perhaps installation of the town's first traffic light in 1984 was symbolic. Change was on the way. Many of those aforementioned landmarks were razed and replaced with sleek new buildings. The Polychronis family's Mount Air grocery store was ousted by a grand new supermarket. Extravagant second homes appeared on the hillsides. Posh Deer Valley Resort introduced elegance to the slopes with opulent skier buffets and valet ski service. And attempts to establish a year-around economy brought about golf courses designed by Arnold Palmer and Jack Nicklaus, racquet and health clubs, and every kind of music, art, and balloon festival you can imagine.

I can't say it is all bad. It has been exciting in many ways and has brought stimulating newcomers, increased recreational and cultural opportunities, and an improved economy.

But it is sad in that we have almost lost our funky little town. No more home-grown rodeos at Ernie Scow's arena where Wayne Putnam, the local garbage collector and radio disk-jockey, used to go daredeviling through a ring of fire on the hood of a car. No made-up rumors about local leaders in the April Fool's issues of the *Park Record*. No clown days on the ski slopes. No walking tours up Main Street with the generously endowed Bea Kummer dolled up in

Victorian dress and picture hat. Perhaps becoming "citified" is making us take ourselves too seriously.

The same thing has happened in just about every small-town-turned-resort throughout the West. Newspapers and magazines everywhere run articles about the spectre of growth. The Aspen story—the transformation of a quaint, isolated, spectacularly beautiful Rocky Mountain village into one of the largest and fanciest ski resorts in the world—is classic. It has occurred in varying degrees of scale and scope in Telluride, Colorado; Santa Fe and Taos, New Mexico; Bullhead City, Arizona; Sun Valley, Idaho; and even the little Mormon town of St. George, Utah, just to name a few. And each community has a model it wants to avoid. Jackson Hole doesn't want to become another Aspen. Park City doesn't want to become another Jackson Hole or St. George another Park City or Moab another St. George. Yet the mold seems set in all of them—unless it can be broken.

As I traveled through Utah, Wyoming, Arizona, New Mexico, Colorado, Idaho, and other states, I conducted approximately 150 interviews of persons in all walks of life and subscribing to varying philosophies. I discovered a commonality that was eye-opening. Even at different levels of development, experiences of the resort towns were strikingly similar. What's more, problems with changing lifestyles, polarized populations, loss of open space and environmental destruction, overcrowding, high cost of living, lack of affordable housing, and eradication of traditional uniqueness were happening throughout the country, not just in the West.

This book has changed since its inception. And so have I. In the beginning I felt genuine concern over the changing face of the American West and hoped to encourage in readers an understanding of its past, an appreciation for what the West really represents in our history and culture, and a strong sense of the importance of protecting this heritage.

But as the writing progressed, circumstances in Park City brought about a kind of desperation in me. Since early 1990, in a period of little more than a year the flood of proposals brought by developers was staggering. The bucolic meadowland in the Snyderville Basin that joins Park City to Interstate 80 erupted with homes. On the north end of this meadow, a monstrous K-Mart store was in progress. Across the street, adjacent to an already-existing motel, service station, and McDonald's, a factory outlet sprawled into the hillside with a Wal-Mart in the works. At the base of Historic Main Street, where the Town Ski Lift traces the old Coalition Mines tramway route up the mountain, plans for approximately 500,000 square feet of lodging and commercial buildings up to seven stories high were placed before city officials. I witnessed the same rapid-fire progression in other resort towns.

Once our precious open spaces are studded with subdivisions and shopping centers, pristine ridgelines marred by luxury view homes, historic buildings razed, and the unique personalities of our western towns wiped out, they will be gone forever. If we don't acknowledge now what is happening and take steps to curb development, in another decade it will be too late.

But there are so many considerations and so many of those western individualists — old-timers and newcomers alike — white-knuckling their causes. Environmentalists, ranchers, resort operators, developers, farmers, real estate brokers, diehards clinging to past ways, tourists and the businesses that cater to them, millionaire second-homers. All have their visions of the future. The philosophical collisions of today are reminiscent of the old sheepmen and cattle rancher wars. I think it is important to understand and respect these diverse and often contradictory viewpoints. Only by identifying and respecting the values that underlie these conflicting goals can we find a way to mitigate the problems of rampant growth. I do see a new mentality evolving as a concern for the environment encourages a philosophy of planned, well-considered growth.

It seemed to me that the best way to avoid repetition in telling this story was to use certain towns to represent stages in the common evolution experienced by all of them. I selected three: Moab, Utah;

Sedona, Arizona; and Jackson, Wyoming.

Moab is a small desert town in southeastern Utah that has not yet experienced the dramatic growth of other areas but appears to be on the cusp of change. It has a long history of boom and bust through a series of nineteenth-century mining bonanzas and ending with the uranium era of the 1950s and 1960s. It serves as an excellent example of a town fighting its way out of economic depression through expanded tourism and attempts to attract outsiders who are looking for an environmentally conscious and health-oriented lifestyle. As well as promoting in-migration, civic leaders are planning retirement communities, educational institutions and cultural centers. Some are even battling environmentalists over the potential exploitation of recently discovered natural resources.

Sedona, Arizona, a small ranching and farming area south of Flagstaff, takes us into the next phase. It hasn't quite reached the stage of massive retirement communities and gated second-home complexes for the designer boutique set, but change is readily apparent. Boasting one of the fastest-growing populations in Arizona, the area is filling with retirees, artists, and New Agers. Touted as a hot vacation spot by travel writers, the traditional agrarian economy has given way to a kind of resortification that drowns any sense of community under hordes of tour buses and souvenir shops. Residents, painfully aware of the rapid growth of Sedona—which was only incorporated as a town three years ago—are attempting to formulate a vision of the future that we will explore in that chapter.

In Jackson Hole, Wyoming, at the base of the magnificent Teton peaks, the transformation from rough-and-tumble western town to glitzy new resort is almost complete. A downtown devoted to tourists, strip developments along the highways, and a new breed of millionaire and movie-star residents all point to the gentrification of a town that somehow hopes to remain "the last and best of the Old West," despite the fact that range-riding cowboys have all but disappeared there. Jackson is one of the best examples of a community in conflict between tourism, ranching interests, a real estate boom, and a determined band of activists trying to curb or at least manage growth.

The final chapters will present the similarities between these three towns together with the other resorts I have visited while researching this book. I will explore the economic and sociological impacts of prices skyrocketing out of range of resident pocketbooks, of polarization between old-time citizens and newcomers, ranchers and miners and environmentalists, as well as the potentially explosive differences in lifestyle and philosophy between free-wheeling vacationers and conservative locals. Finally, I will consider how people are trying to cope with the tremendous changes taking place in the rural West: how community governments are seeking innovative ways to control growth and preserve what is left of their heritage and how citizens can start gaining control over the destinies of their towns.

We are faced with the fact that Americans are departing big cities in droves, each seeking a piece of paradise in the rapidly shrinking frontiers. We must proceed with caution to conserve the unique geography and character of all of rural America, especially the mountain West.

Raye C. Ringholz

one: ON THE CUSP OF CHANGE

There wasn't really a road. It was just a matter of wrestling the Ford V-8 touring car into the wild desert along the path of least resistance. At least he had been wise enough to fit the stock-model vehicle with heavy-duty balloon tires. Without them, punctures from sharp rocks and the probability of getting mired in the deep pink sand would have made the trip miserable if not impossible.

Harry Goulding had figured it was finally time to start showing people Arches National Monument. The strange expanse of natural spires and domes and curving archways reaching three hundred million years back in time had lingered like a wallflower on the doorstep of Moab, Utah, for seven years since becoming part of the National Park System. On June 15, 1936, he took his wife "Mike" (Leone), Laura Tracy, a friend from Vermont, and Moabites Boyd Jorgenson and L. N. Meador on the first recorded automobile trip into Arches since its dedication as a monument.

They started at the highway leading out from town. The open car rattled five miles along a dirt road to Willow Springs, then it bumped and skidded across four miles of boulder-strewn sand to The Windows area. The dusty passengers ignored the baking sun and marveled at the lofty stone pillars and bridges and arched towers. They amused themselves by imagining penguins, elephants, pipe organs, and legendary characters emerging from the picturesque rock.

The next day, Goulding repeated the adventure. This time he invited eighty-three-year-old "Doc" John Williams, Jorgenson, Meador, photographer Harry Reed, and Californian Harry H. Bergman. His enthusiastic passengers spread the word and soon others followed from outside the region.

There had been a great deal of local excitement when President Herbert Hoover signed the 4,500-acre Windows and Devil's Garden areas into the park system on April 12, 1929. But the furor was short-lived. Six months afterwards Black Friday cowed the nation and the Great Depression settled in. It wasn't long before Navajos living in the redrock desert around Goulding's Trading Post, on the Utah-Arizona border approximately 150 miles south of Moab, were starving. The trader and sheepherder, rugged and ruddy as the burnt lands he wandered, wasn't much better off himself. The Indians couldn't buy anything and there weren't many outside travelers coming in to stock up on supplies and admire the rust-colored sandstone monoliths he liked to show them. When the nation's finances started bouncing back, Goulding set his sights on developing some tourist attractions in his beloved canyon country.

For scores of years, there were few who valued the colorful rocky sculptures surrounding Moab for anything other than the wealth that could be extracted from their depths. Mormon farmers who had settled alongside the Colorado River virtually ignored the prehistoric graffiti painted and chipped onto smooth rock faces by the Fremont Indians who inhabited the region around A.D. 650–1250, and the dwellings carved high up on the cliffsides by the later Anasazi. With persistent memories of dismantling their covered wagons and belaying them, piece by piece, down the ragged bluffs to the river crossing, the Latter-day Saints had had their fill of redrock. They reckoned if you couldn't farm or graze on it, it was just in the way.

But the desert didn't seem as forbidding to the turn-of-the-century fortune-seekers. They were game for any hardships if a lode of carnotite was the end reward. Pierre and Marie Curie had discovered the new "wonder element" radium in uranium salts isolated from pitchblende. The same element was subsequently found in carnotite, a yellowish rock on the Colorado Plateau. The news brought hordes of prospectors who flocked into the backcountry seeking deposits where few had dared venture before. On foot, on horseback, with wagons and mules, they dragged out ancient logs petrified into radium-bearing ore. They loaded massive gunnysacks with mineralized rock found lying on the ground. The treasure hunt was so simple that locals could spend a few hours in the hills and return with loot that brought $10,500 a carload. Then World War I called the prospectors to the battlefront and the bonanza came to a sudden halt.

Not for long. Word got out that vanadium, the element prized for strengthening ships, planes, and heavy machinery, remained in the waste dumps from radium-hunting days. Farmers and ranchers again left their fruit orchards and herds to become part-time miners. Outsiders rushed in to join them and another mining craze swamped the agrarian economy. But after a few heady years it was all over and Moabites settled back onto their arid farmlands.

In the midst of all the mining flurry there were a few adventurous nature lovers who continued to explore the backcountry for pleasure, however. One of them was "Doc" John Williams.

"Rawhide John" arrived in Moab in 1896, about two decades after a Mormon community of farmers and stockmen had established a settlement there. He had left his home in Missouri at the age of twenty to join a cattle drive headed for Colorado Territory. Once west, he lived in a cow camp on the site of Denver's present capitol building. Six years later he opened a drugstore in the railroad town of Hugo, where he earned his nickname and a few extra dollars braiding quirts and bridles out of rawhide. He was saving up to go to the Gross Medical College in Denver.

After earning his doctor's certificate he started practicing medicine in Ordway, Colorado—until J. N. Corbin, owner of the telephone company, the newspaper, and a law practice in Moab, learned about him. Corbin figured his town needed a physician more than Ordway and convinced Doc to accept a $150-a-year job as Grand County's health officer. As the only country doctor around, he removed tonsils and appendices, delivered babies, set broken bones, and prescribed and dispensed medications for a variety of illnesses from his drugstore on Main Street. Whenever he had a few hours to himself, he jumped on his horse and rode out to the redrock.

Doc was one of the first to appreciate the beauty and geologic wonder of what is now Arches National Park. He marveled at the towering stone slabs that resembled a New York skyline, a 3,300-ton rock precariously poised atop a natural pedestal, friable sandstone that had been racked by wind and water and chiseled into windows and graceful arches and a collapsed salt valley that dipped and folded in ribboned patterns of lavender, gold, red, and linen-colored sand.

"My father was always talking about fixing up the roads so we could get more people in there," Doc's son Mitch recalls. "I remember in the twenties, Dr. Lawrence M. Gould, a geologist from the University of Michigan, came out and wrote an article about the La Sal Mountains. He always came in and talked to Dad about 'The Windows,' as Arches was called in those days, and they decided they ought to try to get the area set aside as a park of some kind."

The idea would have seemed bizarre to most Moab locals. The roads in town were barely passable. Dirt streets whirled with dust every time one of the few cars chugged by, despite the horse-drawn water sprinkler that attempted to settle the grit. In the broken terrain of The Windows there was nothing but rough tracks that were often boggy from flash floods or piled deep with wind-blown sand.

It was a Hungarian prospector named Alexander Ringhoffer who masterminded events that actually led to the creation of a park. After exploring the northern Salt Valley and Klondike Bluffs areas in December 1922 he got an idea. America's railroads had been promoting tourism since the early days when they organized excursions into "the wild and woolly West" for sightseers and recreational buffalo hunters. They later built European-style resorts at therapeutic hot springs and scenic venues along their lines in order to attract more business. The Denver and Rio Grande Western Railroad operated a small station at Thompson, about forty miles north of Moab, that Ringhoffer figured would be an ideal launching point for tours into the unique country. He wrote his suggestion to the company and in

September 1923 escorted two traffic managers on one of the first automobile trips into the region. The railroad men were so impressed that they lobbied the National Park Service to make a new addition to their system. Six years later The Windows and Devil's Garden, two separate sections in the vast wonderland, were designated as Arches National Monument.

Some residents of canyon country considered the 4,500-acre monument a mere token. Doc Williams and Loren L. "Bish" Taylor, long-time editor and publisher of the Moab weekly, and the newly organized Lion's Club lobbied strenuously to stretch the boundaries to nine times the established size. Harry Goulding joined their cause. In 1938, President Franklin D. Roosevelt added the Klondike Bluffs area to Arches, expanding the monument to some 33,680 acres.

But the germinating tourist industry had barely gotten started when World War II, with its gas rationing and wartime restraints, made recreational travel prohibitive. At the same time other forces were preparing the redrock desert for a postwar boomtime.

Hollywood discovered southeastern Utah. In 1938, Harry Goulding got wind of some new westerns that were in the works. Knowing it was customary in those days to shoot pictures using studio props, Goulding figured it was time for moviemakers to film the real thing. If he could lure producers to his home and trading post in Monument Valley on the Utah-Arizona border, they would find all of the spectacular scenery they could use. And provisioning movie companies would create income for him, jobs for the Navajos, and the produced motion pictures would attract tourists awed by the fabulous natural wonders pictured on the screen.

Taking his last $60 and a portfolio of canyon country photographs, he and Mike set out for United Artists' Studios. Refusing to be rebuffed, they camped on the doorstep until a location director, ready to throw them out, saw the pictures conveniently visible under Goulding's arm. Within hours, Goulding was urging the prominent director, John Ford, to bring his crew to the lodge and promising that in three days he would be ready to service the cast and about one hundred technicians. Ford agreed and brought the legendary good guy, John Wayne, to shoot *Stagecoach* at Goulding's Trading Post.

The idea caught on. Dana Andrews, Ward Bond, Robert Taylor, Judy Garland, Henry Fonda, Angela Lansbury, and Victor Mature followed in Wayne's footsteps to star in pictures produced by United Artists, Metro-Goldwyn-Mayer, 20th Century-Fox and RKO Radio. Ford returned again and again to direct his long string of western epics: *Fort Apache, She Wore a Yellow Ribbon, Sergeant Rutledge, Cheyenne Autumn*. Local students, waitresses, farmers, and Navajos donned cavalry uniforms, gingham frocks, and loincloths to become movie extras. Ranchers rented their wagons and livestock to the film companies for attractive fees. Shopkeepers, caterers, restaurateurs, motel operators, and suppliers from adjacent communities filled their coffers. And Monument Valley's East and West Mittens, Elephant Butte, and Artist's Point were seen by moviegoers through-out the world.

Finally, Bish Taylor and rancher George White figured their town should get in on the action, too. Movie making was good business. So they drove down to Monument Valley to woo John Ford away from Goulding. A few scenic tours of their area in Lester Rogers's robin's-egg-blue Packard convertible convinced the director to give Moab a try.

In 1949, Ford filmed *Wagonmaster* in Professor and Spanish val-leys and along the Colorado River on the outskirts of town. There weren't enough motels to accommodate the crew so a tent village was constructed in the city center. Some of the bigger stars, producers, and directors stayed in private homes.

Moabites didn't know quite what to think about it, at first. But it didn't take the businessmen long to realize the economic benefits. George White built a log stockade and other permanent sets for film-ing *Rio Grande* on his riverside ranch at Castle Valley. Surrogate mountain men, Apaches, and schoolmarms faced the camera for $15 a day and all they could eat. The Arches Cafe served chicken-fried steaks and burgers to movie greats. It looked as though the silver screen had replaced the abandoned vanadium mines and mills as the savior of Moab's failing economy. No one knew that the Manhattan Project of the U.S. Army Corps of Engineers was secretly developing an atomic bomb.

The United States did not have a uranium industry in the early forties. Ore for the nuclear experiments had to be imported from the Belgian Congo or Canada. Small amounts could be recaptured from abandoned vanadium dumps on the Colorado Plateau, but the feds were desperate to find a productive domestic source. While they mined and milled the tailings, they also dispatched scores of under-cover geologists to scour the plateau for new lodes.

In 1945, the deadly mushroom cloud over Hiroshima brought world peace—at least temporarily. But America's quest for uranium was not at an end. A new problem faced the nation; an arms race in the Cold War with Russia. In 1948, to spur the critical hunt for a domestic supply of the ore, the Atomic Energy Commission (AEC, the civilian successor to the Manhattan Project) issued a plea for prospectors to participate in the first federally promoted mineral rush in history.

The fortune-hunters started to arrive: butchers, bankers, C.P.A.s, used-car salesmen, attorneys, and even a few experienced geologists, including one Charles Augustus Steen.

Steen, a skinny twenty-eight-year-old Texan with thinning hair, thick glasses, and a healthy stubborn streak, had been fired for insubordination by the Standard Oil Company of Indiana. To make matters worse, he was blacklisted for life from the oil exploration business. So, when he read about the government's call for uranium prospectors, he deemed it his chance for fortune. Leaving his pregnant wife and three toddlers in Houston, he headed for the Colorado Plateau.

It was a rough two-and-a-half years. The family, with four boys under four years of age, joined Steen on the desert shortly after the baby was born. They lived in tiny trailers and tarpaper shacks. They ate beans, cereal, and illegal venison and sometimes had to feed the infant sugar-laced tea instead of milk. Steen couldn't afford one of the expensive Geiger counters that were considered necessary for uranium prospecting, and he ignored the AEC's guidelines for seeking deposits. Instead, he staked claims according to theories of oil geology that he had learned at the Texas School of Mines and Metallurgy, and tested cores with a broken-down second-hand drill rig. Locals laughed in their beer about "Steen's Folly."

On July 6, 1952, Charlie Steen struck the nation's biggest deposit of high-grade uranium in a geologic formation and geographical area federal geologists had declared barren of ore.

With news of Steen's Mi Vida Mine, bumper-to-bumper carloads of hopeful prospectors rumbled over the forty-year-old, single-lane bridge across the Colorado River and into Moab. There wasn't much there. The four blocks of Main Street ending at Millcreek held a few false-front stores, a bank, the 66 Club, Fern's Cafe, Arches Cafe, the East Side Grocery, and Miller's Co-op.

It was a flash flood of humanity. There were no vacancies in the Utah Inn, Bowden's, or the Apache Motel. People pitched tents along the ditch banks or slept in their cars with no public bathing facilities, no laundry. Hospitable Moabites like Jay Mayhew, imbued with the old western code of helping your neighbor, offered spare bedrooms and sofas to strangers.

Community facilities that had been sufficient for a population of about twelve hundred couldn't withstand the pressure. Electricity, furnished by small diesel and hydroelectric plants, had frequent failures. Water distribution lines were inadequate. Sewers backed up in manholes. The tiny hospital was staffed by one doctor, and Sheriff Jack Skewes and Constable Jimmy King constituted the entire police force.

Yet there was a carnival atmosphere. Steen's excessive enthusiasm was contagious. He bought a fire-engine red Lincoln and flew his dry cleaning to Grand Junction, Colorado, in a private Cessna 195. He gilded his worn-out prospecting boots and built a $250,000 hilltop mansion with a swimming pool, greenhouse, and separate servants' quarters. He was the darling of national media and the toast of politicians and movie stars.

By the end of 1953, city recorder Ellis Foote reported, "The population had risen from 1,272 happy and contented souls in 1950 to upwards of 2,775 harried people and prospectors…"

But the situation was improving. A 44,000-volt electric transmission line was being connected to Utah Power & Light cables. Deep wells were drilled for water. Ore haulers were restricted to driving trucks five miles per hour over the Colorado River Bridge (no gear shifting allowed) while contracts were being let for a modern structure that could handle the loads.

In 1954, Steen initiated a project that promised to insure the economic health of Moab for years to come. By then, America was enjoying the greatest mining bonanza in its history. Over six hundred Colorado Plateau uranium producers were doubling their ore shipments every eighteen months. Eight thousand miners, millers, truckers, and other industry employees collected healthy paychecks. But Steen could see that there weren't enough processing mills to keep up with production. He decided to build one himself. In Moab. True to his nature, Steen's plan was atypical. After securing hard-won approval by the AEC to build the first large independent uranium mill in the United States, he and his partner Mitch Melich succeeded in borrowing approximately $10 million from oft-reluctant New York investment bankers. They raised $2 million more through investors and stockholders, then arranged to build a state-of-the-art plant that would utilize the radically new resin-in-pulp metallurgical process. The Uranium Reduction Company was formally dedicated with fanfare and speeches on September 14, 1957. It appeared that Moab's economy had finally stabilized. But it was a false euphoria. Only five years had elapsed since Steen's bonanza; in five years more the uranium boom would bust.

In 1958, Steen, at the peak of his success, got himself elected as Utah state senator. He spent much of his time at the capitol in Salt Lake City spearheading a state tax repeal and acquiring a county agent for his district. He also succeeded in alienating fellow legislators. Utah's population is predominantly of the Mormon faith. The Church of Jesus Christ of Latter-day Saints subscribes to the doctrine of the "Word of Wisdom," which explicitly forbids consumption of alcohol, coffee, tea, and tobacco. In those days persons who wanted to imbibe spirits had to settle for beer containing 3.2 percent alcohol in a local saloon or "brown-bag" their own bottles purchased at a state-owned liquor outlet.

Steen, a non-Mormon (Gentile in Mormon terms), was about to change the system. He rigorously campaigned to permit Utah restaurants to serve wine with meals and allow customers to purchase liquor by the drink. He also introduced legislation lowering the legal age for purchasing cigarettes from twenty-one to eighteen.

Needless to say, Steen's arguments fell on deaf ears. After three years, disillusioned by the futility of his task, he quipped that he was about to introduce "a head tax on virtue." He resigned his seat in the Senate and moved to Nevada, near Reno, where he built a multi-million-dollar mansion next door to the self-styled castle built by Sandy Bowers, "King of the Comstock." In 1962, he sold the Mi Vida Mine and the URECO mill to international financier Floyd Odlum's Atlas Corporation and virtually broke his ties with Utah.

Things were changing in the uranium industry as well. The plateau had produced almost nine million tons of ore since Steen's strike, and the AEC declared it had enough. Seventy-one million tons of reserves could satisfy the slackening military needs for at least four years, the feds announced. And as for the predicted development of privately owned nuclear power plants, progress was much slower than expected. In 1962, the AEC announced a stretchout program. Until 1966, it would buy only "appropriate quantities of concentrate derived from ore reserves developed prior to November 28, 1958." It was an order that virtually shut down small mine operators. Prospecting came to a standstill. Moabites worried that their bubble had burst.

But in 1960 Texas Gulf Sulphur Company had announced it would construct a $40-million potash mining and processing plant on Cane Creek. While many displaced uranium workers moved out of the area, prospects of lucrative new mining activity encouraged others to await upcoming employment. A road blasted alongside the Colorado River to the mine was in the plan. A $7-million railroad spur with a two-mile tunnel was to be laid all the way from Crescent Junction to the mill. Upon completion of the facility, 220 permanent, high-paying jobs were in the offing. Mining jobs. Work in the Moab tradition.

"Solid money in the bank," said Robert Norman, discoverer of the deposits.

"It will stabilize the economy," city council agreed.

And enthusiasm bubbled with hints of at least six more major potash beds, oil, and magnesium in the vicinity. "Big business is looking our way," Norman said.

They made no mention that Texas Gulf's large industrial building would sit within view of Utah's newest state park, Dead Horse Point.

Oddly enough, there was little opposition to industrialization of this scenic spot. The environmental movement had not yet reached southeastern Utah. Author Ward J. Roylance attributes the apathy to the fact that "Americans in general, and Utahns in particular, were not easily aroused enmasse—in those days—in opposition to such developments in pristine wilderness."

"It was tough for the environmental community," says Ken Sleight, now a prominent Moab activist. "We really didn't know how to speak out. A lot of these things slipped through and didn't get caught."

So construction of the plant proceeded in an aura of unanimous favor. But Grand County's euphoria over this new bonanza was marred by tragedy within hours of Harrison International Company construction crews reaching paydirt.

Workers had spent two years preparing the area for mining by blasting the mountainside, mucking debris, and hauling away waste rock. Then, suddenly, at 4:40 p.m. on Tuesday, August 27, 1963, shortly after the afternoon shift had gone into the mine, the giant headframe rocked with a violent explosion and Ernest Rahaula was blown through the temporary plywood windshield at the twenty-two-foot circular shaft entrance. Flames and smoke raged through the drifts. Methane gas filled the air. Tunnels collapsed. Twenty-five men were sealed underground.

The town recoiled in shock as rescuers, wearing protective orange suits and white helmets, struggled underground to remove the injured and pass communications lines and compressed air to trapped miners. Two black-frocked clergymen paced all night around the floodlit shaft. Eerie green light glowed from high tinted windows of the silhouetted headframe. Eighteen bodies were removed. Only seven miners survived.

The aftermath of grief brought the added hardship of economic breakdown. Surviving employees of the closed mine left to seek employment in other states. Their jobs finished, road-building and railroad crews left as well. To make matters worse, the AECs stretchout program had put the uranium industry on hold. Moab's population which had swelled to about 11,000 with all of the activity, shrank to 4,500.

"I remember we thought long and hard about closing off part of our store and seeing how we could meet overhead costs," Ralph Miller, owner of a local shopping center, remembers. "It was just darned tough times. We cut everything to the bone."

The Moab native never considered moving away, however. His wife and kids pitched in to spend long hours stocking the shelves and selling groceries, hardware, sporting goods, and pharmaceuticals, as the Miller family had done since the days of his grandfather's co-op.

"We always felt Moab had so many things to offer that one of these days tourism would be the thing," Miller says.

Tourism already had a small toehold in the region. It began with the opening up of Arches and expanded when the movie industry and nationwide focus on "the uranium capital of the world" introduced the unusual and colorful rock formations in the backcountry to thousands of people from outside the area. When uranium mining companies graded roads to haul ore from remote places that were previously too undeveloped for conventional access, it became easier for people to take their war-surplus jeeps in to see, in living Technicolor, the surreal country where John Wayne, James Stewart, and Henry Fonda had filmed westerns. The tourists began to respond.

Mitch Williams could see it coming. He had been away from Moab with the Army Air Corps for fifteen years. When he attained inactive status and came home in 1955, the quiet little town he remembered was rollicking in a uranium boom.

Williams didn't waste time getting in on the action. He and his white-bearded, now centenarian father, Doc, operated a trailer court. He started an auto salvage business, piloted Steen's Utex Exploration Company planes, and even did a bit of uranium prospecting. But what he really wanted was to get into the scenic tour business. In 1963, he succeeded in buying a tour operator's permit and Tag-A-Long Tours was born.

Recreational jeeping had caught on by that time. With improved four-wheel-drive vehicles, people were trying to explore the desert on their own. And they were getting lost, breaking down in remote places, missing most of the experience through ignorance about the geology, history, flora, and fauna. Many of them were too timid or inexperienced to reach spectacular places that sometimes entailed backing the jeep around steep, sharp curves or plunging through beds of quicksand.

Williams had a brainstorm. Since people were having trouble driving by themselves, he would lead small caravans of self-driven jeeps into Canyonlands country. The idea caught on for awhile. But pretty soon his clients let him know that they would rather be taken into the desert by a knowledgeable driver in a reliable vehicle and sit back to enjoy the scenery.

The new approach suited Williams just fine. However, his yellow, second-hand jeep couldn't do the job alone. And to afford the necessary fleet of automobiles and equipment, he needed more customers.

So he and his wife Mary got a Small Business Association (SBA) loan and started promoting. They contacted the American Automobile Association and Frontier and Western airlines. When representatives came for a look, local boosters like newspaper editor Sam Taylor, Dr. Paul Mayberry, and Moab Hardware owner Don Knowles helped out. They would pile the scouts into Williams's "Yellow Lizard" and take them into Arches, up to Dead Horse Point, or to see the Indian petroglyphs on Newspaper Rock. Motel operators furnished complimentary rooms. Restaurants hosted meals. Sometimes, Arches National Monument superintendent Bates Wilson feted the guests with Dutch-oven cookouts.

The tourists started coming, but not enough to make the short season show a profit. So Williams expanded with one-day float trips and whitewater river adventures. Eventually, even though he claimed the only foreign language he knew was "Chevrolet coupé," he and Mary attended travel shows and visited agents in Germany, France, Great Britain, Switzerland, and Belgium to entice more visitors to southeastern Utah. Pretty soon almost fifty percent of their clients were overseas vacationers.

Lin Ottinger, another tour pioneer, claims he got into the business by accident. A mechanic with the Army Corps of Engineers during World War II, Ottinger was on his way from Oregon to California for a logging job when he stopped in Boise, Idaho, to see a gem and mineral show. When he spied some rich uranium specimens from Cane Creek near Moab, the dedicated rock hound made tracks for Utah.

"I just happened through in 1956 and thought I'd stay until I'd seen the country," Ottinger says, standing behind the glass counter of his Moab rock shop and touring company.

Thirty-five years later, the lanky, weathered "pack rat" claims he still hasn't seen it all. But a long room filled with agates, quartz crystals, geodes, malachite, dendrites, a smattering of antique sewing machines, ore buckets, car jacks, insulators, old telephones, and a replica of *Iguanodon ottingerei*, the spiny, plant-eating dinosaur fossil he discovered, attest to his persistence.

Antique wooden Indian, Moab, Utah.

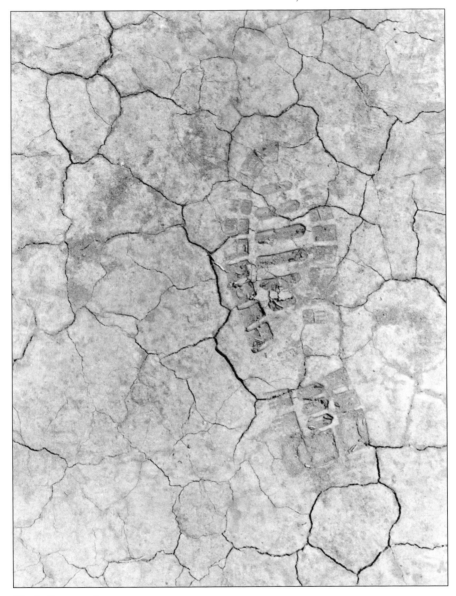

Moab discovered.

Cyclist John Groo on slickrock.

Tex McClatchy, river runner, Moab.

America's most scenic dump.

Pete Plastow, cowboy painter.

John Bicking, saving eagles on the highway.

Art and nature, Tag-A-Long Tours, Moab, Utah.

Ottinger became a backcountry guide when "people kept coming in and saying, 'I wanna go hunting agates. Do you know where I can find agates?'" he told author James Armstrong.

"And I'd say, 'Sure, I know where you can find lots,' and I'd take them out and the wife would watch the store. Pretty soon she was watching it most of the time and getting tired of it. She began pointing out how much it was costing me to take people out like that, so I began charging them for gas, at first, and before I knew it I was in the tour business."

Tex McClatchy also happened into the guiding trade. He came to Moab in 1959 as a schoolteacher but had so much fun "playing on the river" that he decided to take others with him. Leaving the classroom, he bought the first commercially operated jet boats in the nation and skimmed sightseers over the shallow water of the scenic gorge. Thirteen years later, he built a Mississippi-style paddlewheel boat that was hand-launched into the Colorado by the entire population of Moab.

About the time Williams, Ottinger, and McClatchy were getting started, Superintendent Wilson was in the tandem seat of a Piper Cub enjoying his first view of the jagged landscape trisected by the Green and Colorado rivers south and east of Moab.

"There were arches, spires, rugged canyons, crevasses and fins, stitched together with little green grabens," he wrote. "A large number of still-intact prehistoric Indian ruins were visible as I looked down upon the rainbow-hued land. To a park service official, it was the proverbial pot of gold."

Wilson began proselytizing about his dream of a vast parkland encompassing southeastern Utah's geologic marvels. The possibility of their town being bracketed by a national park and monument made the mouths of Moab citizens water. In July 1961 they invited Secretary of State Stewart Udall, Senator Frank Moss, Secretary of Agriculture Orville Freeman, and a party of about thirty other congressmen, reporters, and VIPs to take a five-day tour of the region.

Regional leaders like Sam Taylor, Ralph Miller, and Frank

Wright launched a flotilla of thirteen motorboats into the Colorado River near Moab. The party motored downstream, winding through the goosenecks beneath Dead Horse Point past Anasazi cliff houses, forests of petrified wood, and flocks of herons. They skimmed past high sculptured cliffs cracked like plaid or painted with the mineralized stain of desert varnish. They pitched tents on riverbanks, guzzled Wilson's cowboy coffee, gorged on campfire steaks and fresh-baked Dutch-oven bread. For three days they traveled through the narrow corridor walled by a broken skyline of turrets, gargoyles, and mushroom domes until they reached the muddy confluence with Green River.

On the final leg of the trip, they took to land and sky, hiking remote trails, jeeping into sandstone sanctuaries, and skimming the serpentine canyons in helicopters. By the time they returned to Moab, Udall was sold.

"Acre for acre, the canyonlands of Utah are the most spectacular in the world," he said.

The proposed park not only had the blessing of the Interior Department, but it had a name. President Lyndon B. Johnson formally established Canyonlands National Park on September 12, 1964. Five years later, he more than doubled the size of Arches, which was dedicated as a full-fledged national park by President Richard M. Nixon in 1971.

Still, seasonality posed a problem. In winter, Moab was a tomb. Restaurants, motels, grocery stores, and gift shops suffered along with the tour operators. The town needed a permanent, year-round industrial base.

Uranium made a brief comeback when it appeared that America's nuclear power plants were gearing up in the late sixties. But it was different from the first boom. Ore was deep, necessitating large, expensive drilling equipment. Mining companies had to merge to realize profits. Days of the "little guy" locating and developing small, independent mines were over. It was big bucks and big business from outside the area.

But even the giants didn't last long. Cut-price foreign imports of ore and public fear and antagonism of the nuclear industry—largely a result of the near-meltdown at Three-Mile Island—finally brought the heyday to a close.

Area leaders searched desperately for other ways to salvage the economy. City commissioners proposed expanding the nine-hole golf course and developing a recreation and retirement community on 260 acres of raw land in Spanish Valley. The chamber of commerce advertised for small conventions, marketing sunshine and scenery. Grand County politicos even backed a proposal for a nuclear waste repository to be built near Canyonlands National Park.

But by then an environmental consciousness had surfaced. Attitudes were different than they were in the early seventies when the potash plant announced it would be economically unfeasible to continue operating unless it converted to a new solar evaporation system requiring a number of settling ponds.

In those days, Moabites were all of one mind. They clung to a mining mentality that was based on exploitation of natural resources. There was little resistance to the prospect of a cluster of Clorox-blue pools insinuated on the wild, colorful landscape below Dead Horse Point, so long as the 150 employees of Texas Gulf Sulphur collected their paychecks. Nobody paid much attention to the few newspaper articles announcing the industrial conversion. Opposition came after the fact.

"Environmentalists didn't even know about the ponds until they were built," says author and founder of the Enchanted Wilderness Association, Ward Roylance.

Infuriated that there had been no public hearings or information releases, no environmental impact statement, and no mention in advance publicity that the ponds would impinge on views from Dead Horse Point State Park, Canyonlands' Island in the Sky, the BLM's Anticline Overlook, and Hurrah Pass, Roylance wrote scathing articles in the association bulletin and scores of letters, including one to Governor Calvin L. Rampton.

"Before construction of the ponds, panoramic views from these overlooks swept across thousands of square miles of superb redrock wilderness, marred by no man-made works except some meandering dirt roads," he wrote. He urged Rampton to "use the influence and authority of your office to prevent future recurrences of anything approaching this situation." Rampton complied with an executive order specifying public hearings for any proposed state construction and forming an Ecological Review Board for the Department of Natural Resources.

By the time the nuclear waste repository issue surfaced a decade later, there had been an influx of ecologically minded newcomers to the area. They came explicitly for the small-town atmosphere and the untamed and beautiful country. They mourned for the irreplaceable stretches of wilderness that had been lost to such projects as the potash ponds and construction of the Glen Canyon Dam. And they recognized the necessity for constant monitoring of governmental agencies to prevent further desecration of the land.

Many of these environmentalists were inspired by author Edward Abbey's *Desert Solitaire*, extolling the rugged wilderness and decrying the growing human invasion of Arches, and they related to his fictional tragi-comedy about the Monkey Wrench Gang blowing up Glen Canyon Dam.

County officials found there was a changing constituency in the region. It wasn't as easy to push through a proposal as it once had been—especially to designate a site north of Canyonlands National Park as a repository for some of the Department of Energy's eight thousand tons of spent radioactive fuel.

There were a number of emotional town meetings on the subject in the early 1980s. Within the native stone walls of Moab's historic Star Hall, where Latter-day Saints once prayed and played, arguments flared on the waste disposal site. The proposition triggered a clash of opposing, strongly held philosophies uncommon to Moab. This sudden fracturing of the citizenry was unsettling to a close-knit community oriented to the extractive agricultural and mining industries. Now each faction had its own interests to guard. And no one was about to change anyone else's mind.

The Department of Energy claimed that salt beds in Grand County's Paradox formation could provide safe harbor for high-level waste that had been converted into a solid, glass like substance and contained in metal barrels. The plan called for a series of underground tunnels, each back-filled with salt that had been removed during construction. The repository would be filled in thirty-five years and all surface facilities, except monitoring stations, would be dismantled. The isolated wastes would decay into nonradioactive substances in about 250,000 years.

"The uranium industry is sick," argued Grand County Economic Development Commission chairman Irving Nightingale at one such meeting. Pointing out that Utah's uranium boom days were past, he said, "We're now experiencing twenty-percent unemployment...about five percent move away each year because there are no jobs." Nightingale's contingent emphasized that approximately one thousand miners and millers had called it quits and left. "For Sale" signs had sprouted on every block and business had collapsed on Main Street. Joseph Marcuro had packed up his Indian rugs and paintings and closed Marc's Gallery. John and Jerry Lillibridge had shut down J's Real Wood Shop and taken an $8,000 loss on their home. Unemployment levels had soared to the highest in the state. The repository would create one hundred new jobs and would become a $100 million-dollar industry in an isolated area with few risks to the population.

David Bretzke, director of the Grand County Water Conservancy District, added that selling needed water rights for the Energy Department to operate the dump would generate money enough to cancel a $4.3 million bond issue for a city water diversion project.

"If you can do something to help the economy of Moab, I'm all for it," he said. "Even if it is a nuclear waste repository in the middle of Canyonlands National Park."

But environmentalists warned of hazards such as the fragility of rock surrounding salt formations. They reminded people that Arches' Salt Valley was formed by *collapse* of a salt layer, and that it was methane gas *filtering* through salt that caused the explosion at the Texas Gulf potash plant that took eighteen lives. They argued further that the federal government's abysmal record of dealing with victims of atomic bomb tests in the 1950s left no guarantees that the Department of Energy knew what it was doing this time.

Pete Parry, superintendent of Canyonlands, feared that attendance at the park, which was on the rise, would be threatened. Emphasizing the paradox of talking about establishing hazardous dump sites in the same breath with increasing tourism, he said, "You're playing around with the only thing we have left here. Eighty-nine percent of Park visitors surveyed indicated they would be less likely to return should a repository be built." Chamber of commerce president Dee Trantor added that a waste repository would be a deterrent to a proposed retirement community as well.

The debates raged for months. In the end, a referendum vote defeated the repository, much to the relief of environmentalists and those serving the traveling public.

"It was a battle royal, dividing the community," Ken Sleight wrote. "Peter Parry quietly led the forces in a glorious and victorious campaign against the dump. Also emerging from this was a unification of purpose and community identity."

Not everyone agreed. Long-time residents felt the newcomers were taking over. They weren't so sure they agreed with the tree huggers and developers who were moving into town.

"The old-timers resent the new people some," Mitch Williams says. "They are upset that the whole nature of the town has changed."

Williams, who lives on a hilltop a few miles southeast of Moab, is philosophical about the metamorphosis he has witnessed firsthand. His home is filled with historic photographs, Indian sand paintings, pottery, and artifacts from foreign travels. A large picture window dominating the west side of the house frames a view of a magnificent flame-colored ridge in the distance where colors, blanched and flat-tened in the sun's full glare, gain warmth as lengthening shadows etch bas-relief friezes onto the sandstone walls.

"When that [Atlas uranium] mill closed up, everyone got upend-ed," he says. "People here couldn't get jobs. They had to leave. There were empty houses around, abandoned. Weeds growing up. Some guy who had to leave wrote a letter to the editor and he said, 'Moab is a dying town.' Well, Moab has had its ups and downs, but Moab will never be a dying town."

But Williams admits employment opportunities were scarce. The town suffered from an off-season slump. Those who were not forced to move out had to be resourceful in order to remain. Carl Rappe and the Groff family were among them.

"Everyone suffers in the winter," says Rappe, who has lived in Moab since 1962. "We barely make it…So we looked around and said, 'What doesn't Moab have?' And we did this."

Rappe owns the Main Street Broiler, featuring old-fashioned milk shakes, Cajun fries, vegetarian specialties, thick hamburgers, home-made white-chocolate raspberry swirl, and the only espresso machine in town—all at reasonable prices. The six red vinyl stools at the counter and the few booths and tables are filled from before day-light breakfast until late at night all year long.

"We did this for local people to begin with, not tourists," says Rappe, who wears a Greenpeace T-shirt. Rappe's unique formula has paid off—and triggered competition. "There's been about five more places that opened this spring [1990] basically duplicating what we do," he says.

John Groff and his sons Bill and Robin were other innovators. After losing their jobs in the uranium industry, they looked for new avenues to keep them in Moab. John had been a purchasing agent for Atlas Mines. Bill was a corporate pilot for S&S Mining Company, and Robin worked as a mining engineer.

In 1983, the Groffs hit upon a seemingly radical idea: a bicycle shop. In a mining town! It was before the mountain biking craze heated up and the idea of miners opening a cycling shop seemed pretty bizarre. But Bill was a biker. He liked to ride over the desert slickrock in the nearby hills. He talked his father and brother into pooling their resources, and they got an SBA loan. Rim Cyclery opened shop with four bikes plus a few tires and accessories.

One day the editor and owner of *Mountain Bike Magazine* happened by. Intrigued by the unique biking environment, he published a story about the Groffs, and Moab reached a new breed of tourist. Now the former "uranium capital of the world," is referred to as "the biking capital of the world."

However, Moab's seasonal stigma remains. Summertime tourists don't foster year-round employment. Moabites still seek that elusive "small, clean industry" and wish that retirees and more city-escaping entrepreneurs would move there.

"For years we just had mining and we were trying to develop tourism to go with it. A little extra. The frosting on the cake," says former county commissioner Ray Tibbetts. "Now the frosting is all we have; we don't have the cake."

But Tibbetts envisions something on the horizon. A chamber of commerce poster in the waiting room of his real estate office points to a possible salvation from present economic doldrums.

"WELCOME TO MOAB.

If you like to play here why not stay here? Grand County is looking for aggressive business people who are tired of city hustle and bustle, who would like to move their family, business and careers to a place where there is:

Unparalleled quality of life.

Reliable weather year 'round.

Recreation for everyone.

Clean air—Blue Skies—Open Space."

Perhaps the chamber promotion is redundant. Already signs of urbanization are surfacing. Within the past five years Moab has been rediscovered. Where once arid "poverty flats" and a scattering of small ranches stood in the lowland of Spanish Valley, electric carts putt around the old golf course that has been refurbished and expanded to eighteen holes. A new equestrian center spreads over the rodeo grounds. Graded roads now climb to growing clusters of expensive houses tucked into the juniper-studded mountainsides. Speculators are snapping up investment land in Castle Valley. Two more motels are on the drawing boards and a modern supermarket replaces the former grocery store. There's even a brewery-pub on Main Street.

And at the edge of town a blood-red billboard with the familiar stylized golden "M" beckons, "Come visit Moab's other Arches."

two: PLACE OF EMPOWERMENT

We tried hard to feel the power. We stood at the entrance of a medicine wheel in a small clearing on the steep juniper-covered hillside of Boynton Canyon on the outskirts of Sedona, Arizona. K. C. and I came to experience one of the major earth vortexes said to contain mystical powers that stimulate psychic activity and elevate consciousness. At mid-day, it was warm and still. Sakina Blue-Star, avowed descendent of Pocahontas and adopted daughter of the Cape Cod Wampanoag tribe, brought us to her special place of empowerment to witness her ritualistic dance of the Yavapai Indian maiden, Eh'-ta-wa, who dwelt in northern Arizona long ago.

"The spirits of the canyon won't allow people to come unless they come with the right attitude and motivation," she cautioned. "If you are of good heart, learn to live with the land, and respect the spirit of the land, then you are allowed to be here."

Sakina turned to check the motionless leaves on the shrubbery around us.

"Watch for a soft, almost imperceptible breeze," she told us. "It will be the spirit keeper welcoming you."

Sakina entered the rude circle of rocks. She wore a Lakota Sioux choker of animal bone and long porcupine-quill earrings. A beaded Ute amulet representing the sun dangled on her breast and her graying brown hair was clasped by an Apache headband. Navajo, Hopi, and Zuni silver-and-turquoise rings and bracelets decorated her arms and hands. A Wampanoag ring of purple and white wampum shell glistened on her finger like the metaphysical third eye.

Carrying a sheaf of turkey feathers and shaking a turtle-shell rattle, Sakina chanted in ancient tongues and step-hopped around the wheel. The fringe on her doeskin dress swung and her knee-high moccasins sank in the deep red sand as she twirled and dipped, raising her arms to Father Sky, bowing to Mother Earth.

She knelt to light a bundle of purifying sage smudge-sticks and, as the pungent fragrance rose from the smoke, she laid a small crystal on the center stone.

"Place an object on the altar," she told us. "Retrieve it when you leave and your token will take with you the vibrations of this ceremony and remembrance of this place."

We stepped to the opening of the wheel and asked permission of the spirit keeper to enter. Carefully walking over the rocks dividing the circle into four quarters, we moved in a counterclockwise direction and stopped before a large sandstone slab in the center. I bent down to place my token on the altar: a necklace of colorful wooden blocks strung by my grandsons. K. C., adhering more to the crystal culture, offered her wedding diamond. We backed silently out of the wheel and waited for the magic of the vortexes to overcome us. Nothing happened. Then K. C. saw a sudden puff of wind blow my hair. Sakina turned to face the gentle zephyr and smiled in acknowledgement.

Sakina, like many New Agers, credits mystic energies emanating from the redrock formations held sacred by ancient Indian tribes for drawing her to the Verde Valley. After her physician husband died, she left her home in New England to seek a new life. She considered moving to Aspen near her son and daughter but felt it wasn't quite her lifestyle. She settled on a place in San Diego County but on her way back East to get her belongings discovered the ritualistic Indian lands of Arizona.

"I never made it through Sedona," she says.

Tom Dongo, in his book, *The Mysteries of Sedona: The New Age Frontier*, contends this is not uncommon.

"Sedona has become the recent home to many new, adventurous residents who were irresistibly 'drawn' here," he writes.

Noting the similarity of in-migrants' stories, he claims believers "felt such a strong pull to Sedona that, after a period of time, Sedona became an obsession." They would say, "I quit my secure job, sold my house, said good-bye to my astonished friends and relatives, and moved two thousand miles to a place I had never seen. When I arrived, I felt I had come home."

Not all believers in the metaphysical take on new personas or dress differently than their neighbors, however. Mary Lou Keller, an attractive and fashionable psychic reader from Oregon, migrated to Sedona in the mid-fifties to be around more "seekers." A student of all religions and unhappy with orthodoxy in general, she started her own church called the Metaphysical Center. They met in the local mortuary.

"In those days there weren't any big rooms or halls where we could meet," she says. "The only place that I could find that was big enough was the funeral parlor. Occasionally there would be a viewing of the body on the night that we had our Hatha Yoga class and we would have to move to the jail. There was hardly ever anybody in jail. We said we were going to do our Jailhouse Rock."

Keller later turned her sensory energies to real estate. Claiming there are different vibrations in various locations, she attempts to help clients "find the right place."

"When you go past Bell Rock, you're in the Sedona vibrations," she says. "When you go the other way, you're not. On the outskirts of Flagstaff, vibrations are very calm, peaceful. When you get to Sedona, it's busy, busy, busy, everybody is going, going, going, so we who live here have to get away from it once in awhile just to get rested. Some people can't live near a vortex for very long. Being in the real estate business I see houses going up for sale within a year after they've been built."

The influx of psychics and New Agers is somewhat embarrassing to the rest of the community, however. There is a great deal of publicity when gurus such as Page Bryant, credited with discovering the vortex powers, and psychic Dick Sutphen attract masses of followers to seminars and workshops. Throughout the year notices of full moon ceremonies are posted throughout town. Reports of UFO sightings are common. The Crystal Sanctuary and Healing Research Center offers fire walk demonstrations and classes in Chakra balancing. You can buy astro-numerology charts, have a reading of your past six lives, or take an Earth Wisdom Jeep Tour. There are even smudge-sticks for sale at the grocery store checkout counter.

Lifelong locals like sixty-five-year-old real estate agent Ray Steele don't think there's anything mysterious about the town's rapid growth and debunk New Age claims about metaphysical powers. "A vortex to me was something that the wind current created off the tip of an airplane wing," Steele says. "I'd never heard the term used in any other respect until the New Agers came. Maybe they know some-thing I don't."

Steele claims Sedona has been growing ever since he can remember, and he doesn't attribute it to some kind of spell on the place. The stunning beauty of the surroundings, the laid-back lifestyle, and the affordability of active retirement in a mild climate have attracted most newcomers. "There's a brand new crop of sixty-five-year-olds in this country regardless of the economy," he says, "so we attract our certain percentage who come here and retire. And these people aren't counting on last year's economy; they're depend-ing upon the last thirty years of their productive life."

Different from the erratic boom-and-bust syndrome Moab has experienced since the turn of the century, Sedona's growth has been slow in coming. It started with pioneers like the Thompsons, Purtymans, and Schuermans who homesteaded in the 1800s. The town grew to twenty families after postmaster Carl Schnebly arrived in 1901 to build a hotel and store, grade a rough road following the stagecoach route over the hill to Flagstaff, and name the community for his wife, Sedona.

There was nothing as exciting as a vanadium strike to attract more newcomers. Worse yet, water was scarce and had to be hauled or pumped from rivers. Subsistence farmers grubbed a living selling apples, peaches, sweet corn, berries, and vegetables to each other and miners in the nearby gold camp at Jerome.

The isolated settlement was nestled at the base of a rocky, forested canyon and the only way out to Flagstaff was a six-day wagon trip over Schnebly's rutted dirt road. Automobiles didn't appear until 1910, but it was thirteen more years before gas was available locally. There was no electricity until 1936. By 1939 there were still only about three hundred residents in Sedona and the business district consisted of a wooden schoolhouse, a machine shop, and a small grocery store on Brewer Road and the old Oak Creek Market at the mouth of the canyon. The single telephone line wasn't strung until the 1940s at the same time that the primitive Oak Creek Canyon road was paved, which made doing business in Flagstaff easier and encouraged a few sightseers.

In 1945, the dormant town finally saw a bit of action when Lee and Oma Bird, her brother Paul Adams, and Edgar Page turned the old Oak Creek Market into a combination grocery store, restaurant, thirty-nine-box post office, and tavern. It became the social center of town. Old-timers whom Oma dubbed "The Spit and Whittle Club" used to spend the mornings on the bench out front gossiping while waiting for the postman to arrive. All day long, everyone from mothers with babies to teenagers, grandmas, and ranchers looking for a game of pool gathered to socialize in the tavern. On Saturday nights, the saloon filled with those coming to get their share of the then-rationed beer. Oma even remembers the time a bride and groom in full wedding regalia rode a donkey into the bar.

"We had a place where they could be happy, mostly sit and talk," Oma says. "People didn't get as rowdy in those days."

Other than a few off-the-track travelers and families from Phoenix with summer cabins, the miners from Jerome, the "Billion-Dollar Copper Camp," were the only outside visitors. The hardrockers, who worked four days and had three days off, liked to escape to Sedona for a bit of R and R.

"They'd come out and camp and fish," Oma recalls. "So we had a kind of tourism. Then we had some people going through the canyon;

it [Sedona] was beginning to be known about."

Then, just as in Moab and Monument Valley, Hollywood, eager to capture the vermilion grandeur of the Southwest for a flood of B westerns, introduced the mountains and rocks of Oak Creek to the world. Jesse Lasky had started it all in the 1920s with Zane Grey's Sedona-inspired *Call of the Canyon*, and Hopalong Cassidy galloped through the redrock dust in *Texas Trails*. But in the forties, *Billy the Kid*, *Angel and the Badman*, *Singing Guns*, *Blood on the Moon*, and scores of other films established Sedona's reputation as a major filming location. There was even a German company that arrived prior to World War II to make a western on Schnebly Hill. Locals rumored that the foreigners, who couldn't speak English, were really spies.

The moviemaking provided great entertainment for the townsfolk. After working as extras, wrangling horses, or rousting equipment they gathered to see the day's unedited shoot each evening. "We would go over and see uncut film," former rancher Earl Vanderan remembers. "They showed it outside. We'd sit on logs. There were these men on horses and they had arrows sticking out of their backs. They were riding along talking and laughing, then the cameraman said, 'Action,' and they all stiffened and rode along and you didn't see the arrows. They went up on the ledge and watched for Indians. Then the Indians came out of the woods, slipped up on them, drew bow and arrow, and shot. One of the men would fall over on his horse and there was the arrow sticking out of his back." Sometimes the directors' "creative" scenes put Sedonans to the test. Like the time Vanderan was supposed to drive about thirty head of cattle underneath a waterfall in Oak Creek Canyon. Knowing a few of his herd were ornery, Vanderan didn't water the cows for two days before the scene was shot. They were so thirsty that he succeeded in getting all but one animal under the cascade.

There were no accommodations for the stars and crew members in the early days. They had to commute from Flagstaff—twenty-seven miles away—or stay in private homes until 1946, when D. K. Roberts built Roberts' Deluxe Cabins, Sedona's first motel.

By then the community decided it liked being in the motion-picture business. Carpenter Bob Bradshaw helped fabricate a complete western frontier town beneath Coffee Pot Rock, then stayed on some fifty years as a stunt man, bit player, photographer, cowboy, set builder, and location manager. The Sedona Lodge was built to furnish filmmakers comfortable bedrooms, a huge mess hall, and a catering facility. Later came a state-of-the-art indoor sound stage that locals could rent when it wasn't used on Saturday nights. They would bring their own folding chairs and refreshments, hang a sheet on the wall, and project old-time flicks.

"We called it our Smellerama," Mary Lou Keller remembers. "Right next to the sound stage were the stables. We'd sit there watching the horses galloping across the screen and take a deep breath. It was just like being there."

One of the most famous pictures shot in Sedona was *Broken Arrow*. Jimmy Stewart tangled with and befriended the Apache chief Cochise (Jeff Chandler) at Bell Rock, Red Rock Crossing, Schnebly Hill, and thirty different locations around the area. The multi-million-dollar epic not only showcased the spectacular scenery, but it was also indirectly responsible for turning this Arizona town into an art mecca.

It started in 1948, when Egyptian sculptor Nassan Abiskhairoun Gobran saw *Broken Arrow* in Massachusetts. Gobran, who was teaching at the Boston Museum School of Fine Arts, couldn't believe his eyes as the redrock formations flashed across the screen. Only the day before Hamilton Warren, founder of the Verde Valley School, had shown him photographs of those same cliffs and invited him to establish an art department at his institution. Gobran was impressed by the pictures but had never heard of the place and was not interested in the position—until he saw the movie and the panorama came to life.

"God must want me to go there," he thought.

He decided to try it for one year.

Forty years later, Gobran lives in an unpretentious mobile home

Castle Rock Vortex, outskirts of Sedona, Arizona.

Figures mark a shopping center.

Ken Day, Tlaquepaque sculptor.

Laura Purtyman McBride at Oak Creek homestead.

Oak Creek Slide State Park, Sedona.

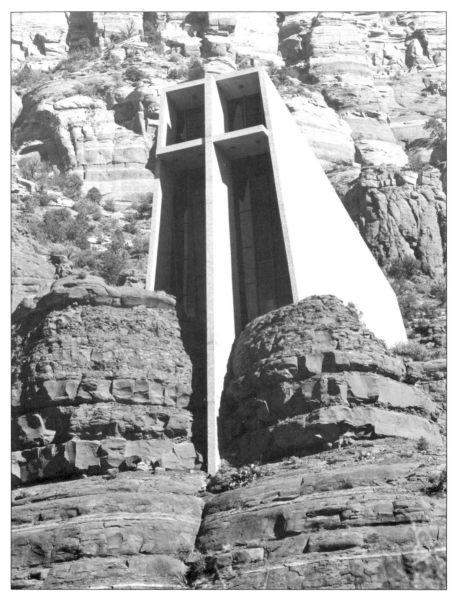

Chapel of the Holy Cross, Sedona.

Sakina's medicine wheel, Boynton Canyon.

Skulls with peppers.

The Vanderans in front of Bell Rock, Sedona.

in West Sedona. One of his lovely sculptures of the madonna and child is displayed in the living room. A scrapbook documents his illustrious career: honor graduate of the Cairo Fine Arts School; representative of contemporary Egyptian sculpture for the International Exposition in Paris; commissions from the Egyptian royal family, the Royal Opera, and the Civilization Museum; set designer for the American premiere of Rossini's *The Turk in Italy*; his works in private collections and museums throughout the world. His proudest accomplishment is founding the Sedona Arts Center.

From the instant he moved to Sedona Gobran knew it was a place where art could flourish. It had already been discovered by Max Ernst, the internationally acclaimed surrealist and a founder of the dada movement in France. Ernst and his new bride, the artist Dorothea Tanning, arrived in 1946. They lived for seven years in a combination studio and home on Brewer Road, where Ernst created his famous cement sculpture, *Capricorn*. When the noted couple returned to France, Gobran rented the studio and accepted Ernst's commission to make a duplicate model of *Capricorn* for bronze castings.

Gobran resigned from the Verde Valley School in 1953 to concentrate on his own career and pursue his idea of creating an art center. He attempted to interest the Museum of Northern Arizona and Flagstaff's Teacher's College but was told, "Sedona is a dead-end place—nothing will ever happen there." Dr. Harry Woods, chairman of the Arizona State University art department, was more receptive. Gobran persuaded him to initiate a summer graduate program in Sedona. It opened in 1956 at the King's Ransom Motel on the site of the old moviemakers' Sedona Lodge.

For two seasons, Gobran tried unsuccessfully to convince Woods to develop a year-round curriculum. Finally, he took the matter into his own hands. He composed a list of prominent persons who might help: George Babbitt (uncle of 1988 presidential hopeful Bruce Babbitt); Hamilton and Barbara Warren of the Verde Valley School; Tony and Marguerite Staude, founders of the Chapel of the Holy Cross; lawyer-rancher Bill Leenhouts; authors Douglas and Elizabeth

Rigby; Eugenia Wright, a local philanthropist; attorney William Stevenson; Helen Varner Frye; Cecil J. Lockhart-Smith; and cowboy painter John Hampton. He prepared his special chicken-and-rice dish and invited the potential board of directors to dinner in the living room of the Ernst studio. By the time the evening ended, the guests had each pledged $50 and their support for the proposed Canyon Kiva Art Center. "It was 1958, the year I became an American citizen," Gobran says proudly. "I appreciated becoming a citizen and I wanted to contribute something."

Encouragement and a few hundred dollars weren't enough to make the project a reality, however. So Gobran set about convincing the chamber of commerce that an art center was the ideal proposition to put Sedona in the public eye. The chamber not only agreed, but member Bud Hummel offered the old Jordan farm's apple-packing barn as a headquarters. The art center could rent the barn for $25 a month and the adjacent house for $75, with an option to buy the two for $35,000.

The board snapped up the deal and pitched in to paint and patch the decrepit structures. They sub-let the house for $100 to defray expenses and on April 28, 1961, the Sedona Arts Center staged a grand opening celebration with an exhibit by Max Ernst, Dorothea Tanning, and Arizona artist Lew Davis. Victor Lombardi's fifty-piece orchestra played in concert and almost three hundred guests became charter members.

Gobran's next challenge was to convince the board to pick up the buy option.

"We rented for a year," he remembers. "The year was almost over and the board of directors was scared to buy it. I said we had to buy the barn. We'd spent about $5,000 to renovate it; we'd lose all the money and not have a home. So the rich people said, 'Where are we going to get the money?' I said, 'We'll work for it.'"

They figured it would take ten years to raise the $35,000. Seven years later, after scores of potluck dinners, entertainments, and fundraisers, the mortgage was burned.

Meanwhile, more and more artists were drawn to Sedona. Sculptress Marguerite Staude spent lengthy vacations at her husband's Doodlebug Ranch. Western writer Bob McLeod lived there. Sculptor George Phippen was a resident. Cowboy artist Joe Beeler and his wife, Sharon, drove through town in 1959 on the way to Tucson and were so mesmerized by the place that they husbanded their resources for two years so that they could move down from Montana.

"Sedona was becoming the hub of many artists' gatherings by the time we arrived," Beeler told author Kate Ruland-Thorne. "Everything revolved around either the Sedona Art Center or our home. An awful lot of artists came through here and we would have a dinner party at the drop of a hat. Our home became a gathering place for such artists as Olaf Weighorst, Charlie Dye, John Hampton, "Shorty" Shope, Gordon Snidow, Grant Speed, George Phippen...you name it."

One get-together had particular significance. On June 23, 1965, Beeler, Dye, Hampton, MacLeod, and Phippen met for a few beers at the Oak Creek Tavern. The juke box at the back of the room blared with heel-stomping music. A seven-foot full-mount of a polar bear towered over a lively crowd. Oma and Lee Bird scurried behind the bar serving drinks. But the artists were in deep conversation. They were founding the Cowboy Artists of America, an organization that would "perpetuate the memory and culture of the Old West."

At the same time Sedona was developing into "Hollywood Southwest" and an artist colony, another event occurred to foster its future growth as a retirement center. The area, as did much of the American West, suffered from a severe lack of water. Being in an upper desert environment, the town's average total precipitation was only about seventeen inches per year. For many years, people were forced to depend on the rivers and creeks for their water supply. Commercial development was next to impossible.

"Water was the reason this area didn't grow," says Oma Bird. "Then about 1947 Carl Williams came into the area. He was really the beginning of everything because he drilled our first good well of water."

The discovery served as a signal for growth. Descendants of pioneers, suddenly aware that their land was more valuable than the crops and stock they were struggling with, sold out to developers who turned the property into residential projects like Broken Arrow and Grasshopper Flats. The Hendley family orchards became Slide Rock State Park. The Jordan's spread was taken over by uptown businesses and it was their apple shed that later housed the Art Barn. Senior citizens from all over the country who couldn't afford the affluent lifestyles of Palm Springs, California; Palm Beach, Florida; or Scottsdale, Arizona, found that in Sedona they could play the links year-round and live in a reasonably priced, double mobile home with a painted gravel yard and a cactus garden.

Don Pratt, a trumpet player from Long Beach, California, was one of Sedona's first land developers. He came on vacation almost forty years ago and returned to invest in saleable property for his livelihood and explore the surrounding canyons for his pleasure. He bought his first piece of land for $6,500 before he even moved to Sedona. A few years later, after he earned a real estate license, he sold it for $9,500. "I thought I did pretty well," Pratt says, "and three years ago a friend of mine said, 'Do you remember the lot you had next to me? It sold for $100,000.' Now they have it priced at $200,000."

There was no construction industry in the valley when Pratt began, so building a home was a major investment. Labor and lumber usually came all the way from Flagstaff. So Pratt planned a mobile home neighborhood in West Sedona "to take care of a lot of people who can't afford expensive homes."

"I don't think any of us are too proud of mobile homes," he admits in retrospect, "yet at the time we had no idea it [Sedona] was going to grow as fast as it did. So we thought there was a need for them."

Later he went on to construct Oak Creek Knolls, the first development with paved streets, and soon became one of Sedona's most active real estate moguls as well as a pioneer in the tourist industry.

Shortly after his arrival in Sedona, Pratt purchased a used 1946 jeep so that he could take his family and visiting friends into the backcountry. The U.S. Forest Service hadn't closed any areas to traffic yet and he explored at will, blazing new trails up the old Jordan Road, around Steamboat Rock, into Secret Canyon, and to the sheer overlook of Rustler's Lookout. He always brought his cornet along to stop at particularly scenic spots and play where the melodious sounds would echo off the canyon walls.

Pretty soon the jeep trips were so popular that Pratt decided to incorporate them into the real estate business. He spent part of the day showing prospective buyers his listed properties, then finished the presentation with a musical tour through back areas filled with wildlife, colorful vegetation, and striking redrock.

It started for fun. Then tourists began trickling into the area, heard about the expeditions, and wanted to come along. Pratt could see he had a winner. He finally bought a small fleet of jeeps, painted them shocking pink like the ones he had once seen in Hawaii, and offered two-hour tours and a complimentary soda for $6. The real estate developer became Sedona's first tour guide.

Abe Miller was a hotel man who turned into a real estate developer. He came to the quiet Verde Valley as a fugitive from the glitz of Las Vegas. Seeking a small place where he could escape for summers and holidays, he bought a cottage in Oak Creek Canyon. He had no idea that he would devote the last ten years of his life to creating one of Sedona's most unique attractions.

Abe's father, J. F. Miller, was equally unaware that he would stay in the dingy town of Las Vegas in 1905 when he got off his Iowa-bound train to take some fresh air. He saw a crowd gathered by the station and strolled over to see what was happening. The Union Pacific Railroad Company was auctioning land. Miller figured some property might be a good deal, as Las Vegas was the only stopping place midway between Los Angeles and Salt Lake City. Impulsively, he scrapped the remainder of his trip and doled out $2,000 for a corner parcel at Main and Fremont streets.

Since there were only two small hotels in town, J. F. decided to build a third. Using the finest materials for construction and decorating, he built the Sal Sagev Hotel (Las Vegas spelled backwards). The hostelry, now remodeled as the Golden Gate Casino and Hotel, became a popular stopping place for travelers to and from the West Coast. And Miller became a millionaire.

Miller's children, Abe and Helen, grew up in the hotel business. They learned the trade, from sweeping floors and making beds to registering guests, and watched Las Vegas evolve from a rustic railroad stop to a glamorous gambling resort with massive neon signs, gaudy floor shows, high-rise hotels, and golf courses on the glittery Strip, west of town. When their parents retired to an Arizona ranch, the brother and sister took over the family business. But as Abe neared his sixtieth birthday, he started to long for the small-town life he had known as a boy. He tired of hassling with paperwork, restrictive ordinances, taxes, and, most of all, deadbeats. He looked for a sanctuary—and found Sedona.

Miller's dream of creating a unique arts and crafts village was spawned in 1971, when his friend Harry Girard decided to sell his four-and-a-half-acre nursery on the banks of Oak Creek below Old Town. Girard was infuriated; all potential buyers wanted to cut down his trees and build ugly apartment complexes. But Miller had an inspiration. He would buy the property and duplicate the charming village of Tlaquepaque that he had seen near Guadalajara, Mexico. As the English translation of the Indian word Tlaquepaque was "the best of everything," he would not only preserve Girard's trees, but would feature three-hundred-year-old carved doors from Mexican churches, hand-forged iron grills, imported tile walkways, flower gardens, fountains, and quiet courtyards. Artists and craftsmen would create their works in the very shops where they were sold. Customers could watch brass and copper ware, jewelry, pottery, weavings, bronzes, oils, and watercolors take form right before their eyes. Art festivals, fiestas, and Christmas pageants with thousands of luminarias lighting the way for traditional processions would make the village Sedona's hub.

Miller's vision became reality in December 1981. He died of brain cancer three months later. The little Mexican art village finally gave tourists a reason to stop a few hours, even overnight, when they made their scenic drive through Oak Creek Canyon. And they were spending money—not just for art works but for food, cocktails, gas, rooms, and souvenirs. Delighted local merchants wanted more attractions.

In 1982, jazz pianist Johnny Gilbert came up with an answer. He convinced the arts center to sponsor an outdoors concert on some property they owned at the old posse grounds. Then he rounded up musicians from Phoenix, Arizona State University, and Northern Arizona University to perform. A stage was constructed and wired for sound. Printed flyers advertised approach of "The Day Sedona Turned Jazz." Tickets went on sale. And the organizers waited to see if anyone would come. They weren't disappointed. Approximately one thousand people arrived with blankets and picnic baskets to savor jazz among the redrocks from morning to sunset.

Former Long Islanders Alfred and Marian Herrman were in the audience. Three years earlier, the Herrmans were vacationing in Scottsdale when a friend suggested they drive up to see Sedona and Oak Creek Canyon. When they started north they had no idea they would fall in love with the place. They were astounded by the redrock skyline and the approximately 2,500-foot-deep river gorge corkscrewing through forests of oak, cottonwood, sycamore, walnut, willow, and alder trees. The unhassled lifestyle and small-town friendliness of Sedona's 2,650 inhabitants also appealed to them, along with the cultural promise of the Tlaquepaque arts and crafts village, which was nearing completion.

They returned the next year to stay a few days. "Just for fun," they looked at some property with a real estate agent. By the time they got home, there was a stack of photographs and descriptions awaiting them. Impulsively, they made a long-distance call and bought a lot they hadn't even seen. They figured it might be promising as an investment.

The Herrmans had no intention of leaving New York. Their children were there. They owned a Long Island jazz club named Tuxedo Junction, where Marian had sung forties tunes with a big band for twenty-eight years. They were accustomed to the pace of the city.

But for three years they visited their Arizona property with its hilltop view of red cliffs and gray-green chapparal. They started to make friends. They watched Sedona's gradual transformation from a modest retirement community to an evolving art center. Finally, they sold the nightclub and built a house on the lot. It wasn't long before their son and daughter followed.

The move was serendipitous. It was shortly after their coming that Marian heard Gilbert's concert and knew she had found her calling. For the next three years the small, energetic woman with a generous grin and sparkling eyes was on front stage belting out songs. The newly named Jazz on the Rocks and a house on Eagle's Nest Lane had become her new life.

If Marian thought she moved to Sedona to simplify her life, she was fooled. She helped organize a board of directors for the annual jazz festival and took over booking duties. Within a few years she was signing up stars such as Joe Williams, Nancy Wilson, Jon Faddis, Billy Eckstein, and the Count Basie Orchestra, who filled the arena with sellout audiences.

When town leaders formed an arts commission, Herrman was appointed as a member. She immediately started pressing for a performing theatre and an Art in Public Places Program to avoid having Sedona be just "a-drive-through-look-at-the-redrock-kind-of-place."

A former commercial artist, she signed up for sculpture classes at the Art Barn. Now a prominent gallery sells her bronzes of jazz musicians, such as "Wailin' Mama" with outstretched arms and a feather boa trailing from her shoulders; the trumpet player straining for a note until his head almost touches the ground; a picker hunched over his banjo.

"I found it [Sedona] more culturally exciting than New York," Herrman says. "There is more intellectual and cultural stimulation, interesting people, no cliques. To me Sedona is a place where whatever is dormant inside of you blossoms like a rose." Herrman doesn't claim vortexes as her inducement for choosing Arizona as a home. In fact, she is concerned about the national publicity Sedona has received for "that sort of kookiness." Still, she doesn't put the New Agers down entirely.

"I'll tell you something," she says. "I have felt a tremendous serenity here. I was magnetized...I mean I lived the same place all my life back in New York and I left everybody and everything and came to live in Sedona. People said, 'What courage.' It wasn't courage at all; I felt I had to be here."

The fact that Sedona's population has compounded steadily over the last twenty years attests to the fact that more and more people passing through as tourists are returning to live. The resident count grew from 1,050 in 1970 to 5,368 in 1980 to 10,255 in 1985 to over 12,000 in the beginning of the nineties decade. And as the town has been "discovered" by tourists and retirees, there has been a subtle change in the type of people in-migrating. While the retirement circuit started with numbers of moderate-income seniors using their life's savings, a more sophisticated and affluent group is building glamorous homes on the hillsides.

It was the mild climate and a touch of "redrock fever" that seduced Bill and Jan Bliss away from Los Angeles and a second home near Palm Springs. Long, lean, and ramrod-straight, the silver-maned Bliss is often recognized as the "Marlboro Man." When he and his wife first saw Sedona in the early 1970s, he was in the midst of a career that starred him in over 365 television and print advertisements for thirteen brands of cigarettes. They were tiring of Los Angeles smog and the proliferation of walled enclaves harboring the cliquish golfing communities in Rancho Mirage. They were seeking a place to retire.

The bucolic little village with a handful of fruit farmers and cattlemen appealed to them, along with the cobalt skies, the bulbous thunderheads ushering short-lived storms, and the weird shapes of sandstone, limestone, and basalt framing the sloping Verde Valley. "Just for fun," they looked at a ten-acre lot with a nice house on it. The package was selling for $110,000. They decided to wait. About ten years later, after retiring and moving to Sedona, Bliss looked at the property again. The price had jumped to $540,000. (The last time Bliss checked on it, the acres alone were going for $1.2 million.)

The Blisses bought a lot in the shadow of Coffee Pot Rock and built a home with a dual art studio, a gourmet-appointed kitchen featuring a restaurant-sized wok, and expanses of view-filled windows. Now, from their exclusive aerie above town they watch the progression of wildflowers changing over four mild seasons. Chipmunks nibble nuts on their redwood decks. Birds and rabbits feed in the oak brush of the surrounding hillside. And a few steps away they hike in solitude where only coyotes and red and silver fox roam.

Sedona natives aren't so sure that things are so peaceful and quiet. Now over twelve thousand residents are settled throughout the greater Sedona area, which encompasses Oak Creek Canyon, Old Town, West Sedona, and the Village of Oak Creek. There are fifty-four art galleries, two nine-hole and two eighteen-hole golf courses, five tennis clubs, and twenty-nine hotels, motels, and resorts, plus six bed-and-breakfasts and forty-three real estate offices. Tour operators offer rides in jeeps, helicopters, airplanes, and hot-air balloons or on horses and llamas. Souvenir stores, Mexican eateries, southwestern T-shirt shops and chic boutiques are proliferating with nonstop traffic on Highway 89A that doubles as Main Street.

Ray Steele remembers when you could recognize everyone in town by their automobile. "You'd always stop to chat," he says. Nowadays it's next to impossible to find a parking space, much less stop in the street to visit.

The appearance of the community has changed as well. Large new homes and attendant power lines and water tanks alter the view of surrounding hillsides. What was once "uptown," where locals socialized at the Oak Creek Tavern, has been given over to busloads of tourists who race through dozens of shops for a few hours and leave. Businesses catering to residents queue up in strips along U.S. Highway 89A through West Sedona or in the Village of Oak Creek on State Highway 179. One doesn't get a sense of solidity with a central-ized commercial and governmental district. The community even straddles the line between Yavapai and Coconino counties.

Citizen concern about Sedona's rapid growth has escalated in recent years. Old-timers like Laura Purtyman McBride, whose grandparents homesteaded Indian Gardens in Oak Creek Canyon, deplore so many new houses and buildings.

"Now you can't see the rocks," she says. "I tried to get a picture of the mountains; I couldn't get anything but telephone lines and power poles...It's really too bad; the place is getting ahead of itself."

More recent Sedonans like Bill Bliss see the need for better gov-ernment and future planning.

"Any time you get growth you get a lot of development that isn't compatible with the surroundings," he says. "The hardest thing to do is legislate taste. Everybody here is trying to keep it from looking like South Lake Tahoe with all the McDonald's arches and Taco Bells. We really haven't got our act together yet."

Bliss and a majority of the citizens feel that the two-county sys-tem and the fact that Sedona was not incorporated as a city contribut-ed to the rather haphazard growth of recent decades. Old Town and Oak Creek Canyon reported to Flagstaff, a university town and the seat of Coconino County. The more populated Village of Oak Creek and West Sedona were administered in the farming country of Prescott, Yavapai County.

"The Prescott area was mostly rural," says Bliss, indicating a disparity between philosophies of the regions. "Here our concerns are [controlling] growth, zoning, preservation of the environment, and you couldn't do that with supervisors in Prescott. They paid lip service."

Over the years there had been several abortive attempts to incorporate, but most of those who had lived under the existing system a long time were comfortable with the old ways and saw no need to "mess with it." It wasn't until the mid-eighties that the idea of incorporation caught fire. Sedona's population had exploded, changed character. Sophisticated newcomers, familiar with urban organization in their former cities, considered the outdated regulations and public services weak and inefficient.

The clash of opinions resulted in the formation of opposing camps. The Citizens for Incorporation argued that jurisdiction by two counties having different zoning and building codes and degrees of enforcement created rather than solved problems. The predominantly rural Yavapai County catered to ranchers and lacked the stringent regulations and planning necessary for Sedona's future, allowing for both urbanized growth and protection of the environment. Under the single aegis of a city government, they argued, new subdivisions, buildings, signs, and roads could be harmonized with the natural beauty of the area. Sedona could control its own destiny.

Proponents also claimed existing police protection and utility services would be quickly outgrown. In addition, a municipal government would be more responsive and accessible to the citizens and would be eligible for state and federal revenues.

Anti-incorporation forces disagreed. They figured incorporation would raise the historically low taxes that had motivated many retirees to move to Sedona. Besides, an incorporated town would be subject to state and federal regulations, such as EPA and other agency directives for sewage disposal, groundwater protection, and so on that the city couldn't afford. In addition, they were aware of some municipalities, such as South Tucson, that had been burdened to the brink of bankruptcy with high premiums for liability insurance.

Primarily, opponents of incorporation wanted to maintain the rural characteristics of Sedona, its distinctive natural beauty, and its freedom from the restrictions of metropolitan life. They didn't want to be citified.

In 1988, after a lengthy and sometimes bitter campaign, a majority of residents voted to incorporate. Predictably, not everyone was happy with the outcome.

"The incorporation has stirred up a lot of antagonism and trouble," says Oma Bird. "I thought we were all right as we were. I was perfectly happy; we had good law people here, reasonably good streets."

Bird and other opponents complain that it was the "Johnny-come-latelys" that imposed their values on the rest of the community and caused all of the problems.

Marian Herrman, who volunteered numerous hours running the petition drive from her living room, disagrees.

"We felt if we wanted to preserve our way of life and our beautiful place, we had to do something about it," she says. "It's nice to be able to make a difference."

With three years of incorporation under the city's belt, a project to construct a much-needed sewer system is underway and a series of town meetings to hear persons from all of the various persuasions has been conducted to lay the groundwork for a new master plan. But the spectre of an ever-expanding population hasn't gone away. In fact, Sedona is entering the next growth phase where wealthy second-home owners from the East and West coasts drive up real estate prices.

"Growth of Sedona is more word of mouth," says Frank Miller, a Sedonan and executive director of the chamber of commerce for less than two years. "I often say we could almost cut out any type of publicity about Sedona and tourists would still be coming.

"The main problem is how many people can Sedona absorb and still remain relatively free of pollution, traffic problems, and building condos in the side of the Forest Service land. It's a matter of controlling growth, not that there should not be any."

As to how the new city council is going about that, Miller admits there's still a lot of policy shifting.

"One step forward and two steps back," he says. "Growing pains."

three: HOW THE WILD WEST WAS LOST

"We've seen a lot of changes," Jack Huyler says. We sit on the front porch of his spacious log home at the Rocking H Ranch in Moose, Wyoming, in Jackson Hole, a few miles west of the town of Jackson. A field of wild yarrow, golden columbine, and periwinkle-blue fleabane blooms among a scattering of outbuildings on the secluded grounds. A narrow corridor through the lodgepole pines frames the glacier-ridged Teton peaks in the distance. All is quiet but for the sounds of Margaret Huyler puttering in the kitchen. It seems remote and improbable that the Teton Village Ski Area and Teton Pines Resort Community with its championship golf course, racquet club, and acres of lavish homes are just across the road.

"Come inside and I'll show you a photograph of Jackson the way it was when we were kids," Huyler says.

We enter a rustic living room dominated by a massive rock fireplace stained with the smoke of many welcomes. A picture taken in 1926 hangs beside the front door. It shows a few log cabins, frame shacks, and false-fronted buildings of locally made brick centered in a remote valley dotted with small homesteads and ranches. A black water tank on high stilts towers in the distance. Weathered boardwalks surround a scruffy Town Square with a tall flagpole sprouting from a rocky field of sagebrush. East of the square is the Gun and Commercial Club clubhouse, where dances were held on the second floor and the Jackson Drug Company dispensed malts and medicaments at street level. There was Billy Mercill's General Merc. The Crabtree Hotel. The Wort family's winter cabin. "Old twelve-percent" Miller's Jackson State Bank. "Pap" Deloney's Mercantile, farm implement store, and candy den.

Huyler, who retired twenty years ago from teaching at the Thatcher School in Ojai, California, lives on fifty acres of his family's former cattle ranch where he summered as a boy.

"I don't think the prewar days were the good old days," he says. "I think if Jackson had stayed as it was then I probably wouldn't have retired here. But the postwar years, the fifties and sixties, were excellent. I haven't put a calendar on it but some of the things have changed for the better. Introduction of rural electricity, which we hadn't had here. The advent of over-the-snow equipment and four-wheel drives. Down clothing and all made the winters a lot better. It kept the valley from getting so introverted and closed in as it had been in the old days."

The broad valley of Jackson Hole has been a summer place since the 1800s, when it was crisscrossed by Indians and fur-trading mountain men like John Colter, Jedediah Smith, Jim Bridger, Thomas Fitzpatrick, and William Sublette, who named the "hole" for Davey Jackson.

Around the turn of the century it became a seasonal mecca for American millionaires and European noblemen. They organized elaborate expeditions to climb the Tetons, pull cutthroat trout from the lakes and streams, and hunt the abundant elk, deer, antelope, and moose. The few year-round settlers, who had been attracted by the plentiful water and luxuriant grasses, began taking time from cattle ranching chores to act as hunting guides and outfitters. With the brief growing season, harsh winters, and unstable beef market, dude wrangling soon became more than a method of supplementing their incomes to tide them over until spring.

As the popularity of dude ranching grew, others opened facilities geared specifically to the visitors. Ray Hamilton and John Sargent constructed Merymere, a beautifully furnished cabin for ten guests on the shores of Jackson Lake. Stephen Leek established a hunting camp. Ben Sheffield built another cluster of log houses at Moran. Finally, in 1908, Louis H. Joy and author Struthers Burt opened the

Contemporary version of a traditional western symbol.

Jackson's town square.

Historic Jackson Drug Store.

Saturday night at the rodeo.

Snow Park Resort, Jackson, Wyoming.

Snake River.

Virginia Huidekoper.

Shoot-out on Jackson Square.

Jackalope, a western folklore tradition.

Moose, Wyoming.

first authentic dude ranch, the J-Y, on Phelps Lake. A new industry was born.

"In its typical form it [the dude ranch] is a genuine Western stock ranch whose accommodations have been amplified to entertain a number of vacation guests—honorably entitled 'dudes' in Western parlance," the Union Pacific Railroad wrote in the promotional pamphlet, *Dude Ranches Out West*.

Regional author Donald Hough had a different characterization of the city folk.

"A dude is one who comes in for weeks or months, stays at a dude ranch or something like it, dresses more like a cowhand than a cowhand does, and in a kind of simpleminded way tries to fit into the country. The dude is in the minority (compared to the tourist)—he, and especially she, takes up little space except when sitting down."

By the mid-1920s, the concept of dude ranching had caught. Vacationers would take the train to Ashton or Victor, Idaho. There, by auto stage, they drove to outfits like Castle Rock Ranch, "A Home Away from Home," and the thousand-acre El-Bo Ranch that encouraged "greenhorns" to help wrangle stock and pitch hay.

Top of the line was the Bar B C, where invited guests could "rough it in comfort" with hot water and portable tubs for $300 per month or $77 a week, including horseback riding. The requirement of personal references for prospective guests was "a policy strictly adhered to."

Besides being "a ranch owner, a cowman, a horseman, a guide, a wholesale chambermaid, a cook, and storekeeper rolled into one," the new breed of ranchers were among the first preservationists—of both land and animals.

When the raging winter of 1909 killed half of the elk that had migrated from Yellowstone, the ranchers provided what hay they could spare to feed the starving herd. Finally in 1911, the state of Wyoming and federal government joined in an artificial feeding program. A year later Congress authorized purchase of 1,760 acres in the Flat Creek area for a national elk refuge. In succeeding years, additional federal purchases and private donations of lands by the Isaac Walton League and John D. Rockefeller, Jr., expanded the refuge to its present 24,000 acres.

It was as if the ranchers were appreciating the country for the first time through the enthusiasm of their guests. The magnificent surroundings and milling herds of wild game that they had always taken for granted suddenly represented money in the bank. Enjoying the best of both worlds, they could graze their stock and cash in on the growing tourist trade at the same time.

The ranchers' conservationist mode was short-lived. Their attitudes began to change as rumors flew that Washington might adopt the Teton region into Yellowstone National Park.

Ever since 1882, when General Philip Sheridan first broached the idea, the concept of tying Jackson Hole into Yellowstone, America's first national park, had been explored. After a national surge of conservation programs in the 1890s had created the Yosemite, Sequoia, and Mount Rainier parks, Colonel S. B. M. Young, acting superintendent of Yellowstone, recommended that his authority be extended to include Jackson Hole. He and other concerned citizens deplored the fact that Jackson's wildlife and natural beauty were not receiving protection equal to that available under his jurisdiction. Local dude ranchers also feared that, out of economic necessity, the growing numbers of homesteaders might begin developing the pristine country. They deemed the best way to insure its protection was to incorporate the land into Yellowstone.

As the decade neared its end, a number of bills came before Congress but elicited only mild support. It wasn't until 1915, when Stephen Mather, director of the National Park Service under Secretary of the Interior Franklin K. Lane, and his assistant Horace Albright first viewed the Teton peaks, that someone took on the preservation of the scenic gems as a mission.

For two years, Mather and Albright worked on formulation of a feasible plan for the park. In April 1918, after extensive consultations with the Wyoming congressional delegation, they joined with

Congressman Frank Mondell in authoring a bill to extend Yellowstone's boundaries. Mondell introduced a slightly revised bill in December which found unanimous support in the House the following February.

But when the proposed legislation reached the Senate, Idaho Senator John Nugent was against it. Since the bill required unanimity to reach a vote and the Senate was in filibuster at the time, Nugent succeeded in stalling the presentation and killing the proposal.

Park advocates later discovered that Idaho sheepmen had learned that the amount of land in the proposed extension available for grazing had been reduced. The irate ranchers had figured that the cut had been ordered by the U.S. Park Service. In retribution, they lobbied Nugent to defeat the Park Service bill.

In actuality, it was the U.S. Forest Service that had issued the directive for grazing limitations. There was a great deal of competition between the two federal agencies regarding the administration of the land in question. Although chief forester Henry S. Graves had made no official pronouncement, his private comments against the park extension were well known. Mondell and his colleagues felt it was more than coincidence that the grazing quota was put into effect when their bill was introduced.

Inspired by their Idaho colleagues' success, Jackson Hole ranchmen decided their collective body could be a viable political force, too.

According to author Robert W. Righter, "Whatever the facts of the park extension regarding grazing rights, the livestock interests opposed in principle further federal control. Ever since the beginning of government restrictions on the public domain in the 1880s, cattlemen and sheepmen felt hounded by Washington administrators who knew little and cared less about their problems."

Mondell's bill had had other opponents. The dude ranchers, independent westerners to the core, had also rebelled at the idea of federal regulations. Spokesman Struthers Burt lashed out at Park Service policies on concessionaires that favored monopolies, eliminated competition, and discouraged private enterprise and personal initiative. In addition, dude wranglers objected to all the restrictive red tape and stringent regulations the agency imposed. They didn't want signs telling them where they could or couldn't camp or dinky little paths restricting their hikes and horseback trips.

Disappointed that Mondell's bill never made it out of committee after being reintroduced in May 1919, Albright, who had since been appointed superintendent and dubbed "the Duke of Yellowstone," returned to his post. Undaunted by the setback, he commenced a campaign of introductory tours for VIPs on the political and writing scene to come and see the country for themselves. He also engaged in a new battle with the Forest Service.

In 1918, President Woodrow Wilson, anticipating passage of Mondell's first bill to enlarge Yellowstone, withdrew six hundred thousand acres from within the Teton National Forest with the intention of including it in the proposed park extension. Although Mondell's bill didn't pass, the executive order was never rescinded. The action essentially gave the Park Service final review power over any Forest Service disposition of that land. L. F. Kneipp, chief forester at the time, protested the divided responsibility to no avail. The situation only served to inflame the rivalry between the two agencies.

The conflict came to a head in the 1920s when Albright vetoed a water storage project that had been approved by the Forest Service on Two Ocean and Emma Matilda lakes. He deemed that the imposition of a dam on the environment would be detrimental to the park. The district forester had no recourse but to concede Albright's veto power. The project was scrapped.

Jackson's dude ranchers cheered Albright's stand. They had begun to worry that the untouched country that attracted their guests would be overtaken and ruined by unsightly tourist development. Since the Forest Service, Jackson residents, and the cattlemen evinced little concern for preservation, Burt and his cohorts figured the Park Service was the least offensive ally. They still didn't like all of the restrictions, but they were better than too many dams and lots of honky-tonk roadhouses and souvenir shops.

The fragile relationship was consummated on July 26, 1923, when Struthers Burt and a few other Jackson Hole dude ranchers and businessmen invited Albright to meet with them at Maud Noble's cabin. Gathering in front of the fireplace, they drew up plans for a recreational area. Burt called it a "museum on the hoof." There would be protection of indigenous animals, log buildings, and unpaved roads, and Jackson would be preserved as a frontier town. They would try to interest private investors in purchasing the northern portion.

The gathering of these dedicated preservationists bore fruit. In 1924, John D. Rockefeller, Jr., took a family vacation in Yellowstone. When he returned two years later, Albright hosted the millionaire on a twelve-day tour of the park and Jackson Hole. They picnicked, watched moose slosh through the marsh, visited dude ranches—and saw ugly shacks, telephone wires, and even a squalid dance hall beginning to encroach on their view of the Teton peaks.

Albright told Rockefeller about the meeting at Noble's cabin.

By wintertime, the superintendent was in New York with maps and reams of information. He proposed that John D. buy about fourteen thousand acres on the west side of the Snake River for around $397,000. Rockefeller agreed and added purchase of another hundred thousand acres on the east side of the valley for a little over $1 million. He specified that the land eventually be turned over to the federal government as part of the National Park and National Forest systems.

Euphoric with success, Albright suggested that the Rockefeller negotiations be kept under a veil of secrecy. If ranchers knew who was behind the offers to buy their property, the prices would go sky-high. He advised the millionaire to create a front organization disguised as a recreational and hunting club to handle the purchasing negotiations. The Snake River Land Company was formed for this purpose.

At the same time that Albright was dealing with Rockefeller, Congress was waging a continuing debate over whether to extend Yellowstone Park into Jackson Hole or establish a new park. In February 1929, Wyoming Senator John Kendrick finally succeeded in passing a bill to create Grand Teton National Park. President Calvin Coolidge promptly signed it into law.

The new park left much land under the aegis of the U.S. Forest Service. Neither Albright nor Rockefeller's conservation group was entirely pleased with the designation. Historian John Ise described it as "a stingy, skimpy, niggardly little park of only about 150 square miles." But Albright knew his secretive land deals could change the picture.

So now there were two national parks in Wyoming back to back, with grizzlies and geysers, serrated snow-capped peaks, and glacier-fed lakes. Roads were paved and trails cut through the pines. Motels, filling stations, and souvenir shops sprouted in Jackson to serve the 1.5 million-plus drive-through tourists replacing the dudes who had stayed months at a time.

The town of Jackson put on a show for the visitors. The place went wild on Saturday nights. Local wranglers bucked on broncs and bulls at the rodeo grounds. Fistfights followed. Then everyone trooped downtown to the Wort Hotel, Cowboy Bar, or Log Cabin. Beer caps popped. Cowboy music twanged. Croupiers raked in the chips at crap games and roulette tables. Slot machines spewed clanging silver. Nobody cared that gambling was illegal in Wyoming.

But at the first snowfall, everyone went home.

Hibernating locals stocked supplies and waited to be "snowed in" until spring. Cash was tight during the long, cold months and there was little to do for recreation. They filled the time with dog or cutter racing on Main Street, ice skating on Jenny Lake, and all-night poker games.

"This was a totally depressed area in the winter," Jack Huyler remembers. "All people had to do was go into the bars and drink unless they had ranches and were running cattle. They lived on the cuff all winter and the first part of the summer had to pay off their debts for bills they'd accrued."

In the mid-1920s, forester Mike O'Neil provided Jackson Holers a new winter diversion by constructing a ski jump on the hill south of town. Mike got the local blacksmith, C. H. Brown, to fashion iron toe holds and strap holders for his wooden skis and some metal points for the bamboo fishing rods he used as poles. Soon other local athletes were struggling to herringbone up the hill and become airborne with O'Neil. Jumping matches became a popular winter pastime.

By 1933, O'Neil's pioneering had caught the fancy of community benefactor Ruth Hannah Simms. Despite the fact that there was still no uphill transportation, she donated money for the Jackson Winter Sports Association to build a proper jump on the mountain overlooking town. Four years later, the newly formed Jackson Ski Club initiated competitive Nordic and Alpine meets on Simms's jump and a few rustic runs that had been snow-packed over hiking and horse trails cleared by the Civilian Conservation Corps.

The Snow King Resort, Jackson's first real commercial ski area, opened in 1939. And there was good news for skiers weary of climbing up the mountain on their own power. The owners had paid a Casper, Wyoming, oil-drilling company $500 for a used cable tow and hooked the line to an old Ford tractor. Skiers could clamp a wrench onto the cable and hold onto an attached rope and wooden handle that would pull them up to the top. Local support of the ski mountain was enthusiastic. But only a few outsiders were game enough to wrestle winter roads into the isolated valley. Former Utahn Virginia Huidekoper was one of the stalwarts.

"We heard about this big ski meet in Jackson Hole," she says. "There was a group here that wanted to get the skiing started. They sent invitations to people in Idaho, Utah, and Wyoming. We thought we were going to Antarctica, it seemed so remote. It was lovely. It was so small and I remember the snow was plowed up along the streets with an aisle next to the buildings. It was a marvelous sort of holed-in-for-the-winter feeling."

Huidekoper was entranced. She returned several summers to visit friends. Then one fall, after she and her husband Jim had climbed Mount Owen, she couldn't bear to leave.

"The geese were flying over," she remembers. "Everything was turning and there was wood smoke here and there. We thought, 'Wouldn't it be neat to try a winter here.' So we did."

Huidekoper's long winter has never ended. Since divorced, the former editor of a weekly newspaper, author, sportswoman, and professional pilot now lives alone on a two-hundred-acre alfalfa ranch in the woods beneath Teton Pass.

World War II brought Jackson's activity to a near-standstill. Automobile travel was virtually cut off until peace and the end of gas rationing allowed waves of fun-starved vacationers to return. Once the highways began to fill, sales tax revenues doubled, property values tripled, and the old cow town started to put on a new face.

It was 1956 when Californian Paul McCollister asked his wife how she would feel about a permanent move to Wyoming. They were perched on a buckfence at their summer ranch in Moose, sipping cocktails and listening to the twilight burst of evening sounds. They had owned their ten-acre spread in Grand Teton National Park for four years. McCollister was forty and ready to retire on his sizable savings from investments in a radio advertising agency and a subsequent partnership in the San Jose *Shopping News*. He had discovered Jackson on a hunting trip in 1942 and had come back a few years later to fish. He finally bought the ranch in 1950 and knew he was home.

"How would you feel about pulling out of California and moving here?" he asked her.

"Fine with me," she said.

The following year, officially retired, they moved. And experienced Wyoming winter and skiing on Teton Pass and at the little Snow Park Resort overlooking town.

Since the end of World War II, skiing had evolved as a national sport. Growing lines of slatsters boarded complexes of ski lifts skimming up the mountains of played-out western mining towns like Aspen, Colorado; Sun Valley, Idaho; and Alta, Utah. In 1945, Jackson's Winter Sports Association built a new four-thousand-foot-long single chairlift on Snow King Mountain, a modest conveyance reconstructed from the "Lilly," an ore tramway scrounged from the abandoned gold mines of Garfield, Colorado.

A few other Jackson Hole locals started talking about connecting with America's exploding ski mania. Bill Jensen and Bill Ashley, owners of a sporting goods store, wanted to promote a new resort on Cache Creek, a few miles beyond Snow King Mountain. They talked their friends Hugh Soest, Louis Dopyera, Paul Van Gontard, and Jim Huidekoper into investing in the project. Paul McCollister judged the prospective terrain "either steeper than a cow's face or flat—no in-between to speak of"—but finally agreed to join the partnership and become chairman of the Jackson Hole Corporation.

But McCollister pulled out of the corporation after a feasibility study by Willy Schaeffler, head ski coach at the University of Denver, confirmed his original suspicions of the area's unsuitability for skiing. Besides, he had found a better place to build a resort on the high peaks above the Crystal Springs Ranch in Moose. In 1963, Schaeffler completed a study of snow conditions in that area over four winters and proved McCollister right. He reported that the six square miles of skiable terrain was superb.

It was in 1961, after spending a year in Europe, that McCollister met the enthusiastic developer, Alex Morley. Morley, a Cheyenne, Wyoming, building contractor and banker, had taken early retirement that year and settled in Jackson. He had been considering promoting his own ski resort on Buck Mountain, south of the three Teton peaks. When he met McCollister, it didn't take him long to change his mind when his future partner rhapsodized over the recreational potential of Rendezvous Mountain on the southern flank of the Teton Range. It had an impressive vertical rise of 4,135 feet, great bowls of powder snow, and it was close to Jackson, which by now was a thriving summer tourist town with an airport and all-weather highways.

The big problem was financing the project.

Although Jackson's summer business flourished, the partners realized that winter remained a long season of economic depression. So when McCollister saw an article in the *San Francisco Chronicle* telling about the Federal Area Redevelopment Administration (FARA) program to aid communities that suffered from a seasonal economy, he figured that was the answer. He and Morley enlisted the support of then-governor Cliff Hansen to help them qualify for the assistance, and together they succeeded in getting a special bill through the legislature allowing the state to participate. Bringing in Gordon Graham, McCollister's partner from California, the trio formed the Teton County Development Company.

According to McCollister, the partnership hoped for a $975,000 FARA loan to help capitalize the $1.6 million undertaking. But shortly before Christmas, Senator Gale McGee called him and said, "Paul, how would you like a $1 million-dollar Christmas present?" With this unexpected windfall from the feds, Teton Village Ski Resort was on its way.

Teton Village opened in 1965. *Western Ski Dealer Magazine*'s April issue enthused: "A brash, young and ambitious newcomer will take its place among the West's major league ski resorts next winter backed by all the size and muscle necessary to make it a winner."

Olympic gold-medalist Pepi Steigler was hired to run the ski school. The largest ski aerial tramway on the continent was constructed to speed loads of sixty-seven winter sportsmen and summer sightseers 12,500 feet to the top of Rendezvous Mountain in a little over six minutes. There would be three double chairlifts the second year of operation.

The ski area marked the beginning of a year-round tourist season for Jackson Hole and also attracted a different clientele from the family-oriented vacationers who made the summertime Yellowstone-Jackson loop. Generally more affluent, the ski crowd demanded luxurious accommodations and aprés-ski excitement when the lifts closed. The Village responded with Alpine-style hotels featuring bars with live entertainment, fancy restaurants serving hot mulled wine, beef fondue bourguignon, and champagne brunch buffets instead of Jackson's usual beer and chuck-wagon barbecues.

Still, with traffic-choking blizzards and national economic recessions during the first eleven years, the ski corporation lost $2.5 million on lift operations alone. Morley and Graham finally sold out to McCollister.

McCollister recognized that real estate development was the most profitable segment of the project and could be the quickest route out of the red. Nineteen residential lots had already been sold. One, with an impressive price tag of $12,500, was even purchased before the resort had opened. McCollister didn't stop at Teton Pines. Once the ski area was underway, he started on an 18-hole golf course and exclusive 160-lot residential community near the airport. So when the resort appeared to be in trouble, he expanded the original master plan for his quaint European village by including 40 commercial pads, 120 wooded sites for private homes and condominiums, and additional lodges. His promotions were prophetic of things to come.

"The ski resort started building in '62," says Virginia Huidekoper. "That was the first time we ever heard of a lot for sale for $12,000. That changed the price of everything. Suddenly homesites were coveted."

For awhile, the resort didn't seem to have much direct impact on the town itself. Most shopkeepers, motel owners, and restaurateurs still closed for the winter. Many residents left the area for warmer climes. Long-time Jackson Holer and former chamber of commerce director Mickey Waller saw little effects on the community for the first eight or ten years.

"I was out of the valley from 1974 to 1982 when the big change came," she recalls. "I would come back each summer on vacation and could not believe my eyes of the changes in a year's time. When I left, the town went out as far as the Sagebrush Motel, and that was it. There was nothing beyond that. By the time I came back in '82 it had started down south...the Aspens, Rafter J, Skyline developments."

A significant alteration was the loss of stock and alfalfa ranches gracing Jackson's entry corridor. The situation had changed for the stockmen who had once been predominant. The livestock business wasn't what it used to be. They were fighting low beef prices and what they considered to be excessive government control on grazing rights. As development encroached upon their property it became harder to stay in the cattle-raising business and to resist tempting offers for their land.

But it was not just cattlemen selling out. Numerous old-timers, weary of traffic congestion, heavy weather, and loss of a cow town atmosphere, succumbed to tantalizing offers for their homes.

"The little house their dad had left them and a piece of land probably cost $25–30,000," says Mickey Waller. "They'd add a room as each kid came. Then all of a sudden they were sitting on $500–600,000. So they sold and went someplace they thought hadn't been despoiled yet. A lot moved to Whitefish, Montana."

At the same time, Jackson became a target for those escaping the hazards and hectic pace of big cities. The new subdivisions started filling with people who came, not because employers had transferred them or they were returning to their roots, but just because they wanted to live in Jackson Hole. The town's population expanded from 2,688 residents in 1970 to over 5,000 in 1990. In twenty years, Teton County exploded from 4,823 persons to more than 13,000. It was an interesting and diverse group of newcomers, encompassing artists, retirees, musicians, ski bums, and budding entrepreneurs.

And tourism went wild. Almost 1.5 million people visited Grand Teton National Park in the summer and over 400,000 came to ski in the winter.

Physical transformation of the area during the 1970s and early 1980s was far-reaching. Downtown Jackson, an area touted by the chamber of commerce as "the last and best of the Old West," started to change. Small mom and pop businesses gave way to chains and franchises. One of the first hit was the Jackson Hole Mercantile that had been dispensing hardware, toys, furniture, and other necessities on Town Square for almost fifty years. One of the employees bought the store from his boss just before the 40,000-square-foot Pamida discount center opened south of town. The merc was closed out within a year.

Howard Ballew and Bud Walters's B & W Market on the northeast corner of the square grossed almost $1 million a year until Saveway (later Thriftway) opened in a shopping mall with a big parking lot and B & W closed their doors. Finally Safeway built a huge supermarket that broke them all.

The Teton Gables Cafe had been a popular spot since the 1940s. Then came McDonald's in the early eighties and another local was closed out.

The invasion of chains continued. Lumley Drugstore succumbed to Albertson's pharmacy. The Open Range Restaurant became a Ralph Lauren outlet. The neo-art-deco Cadillac Grille ousted the Silver Spur. The Sizzler came to town. Wendy's. Kentucky Fried Chicken. Even a wax museum.

As a result, real estate prices ballooned and taxes soared. The new population swelled and demand for moderately priced housing increased. Long-time residents like Kelly and Shelley Rubrecht were adversely affected.

"After thirteen years as model tenants—paying our rent on time,— improving the property—we were kicked out," Shelley said over a glass of wine at the Silver Dollar Bar of the Wort Hotel. "Just like that!"

The Rubrechts were spitting mad. Their landlady had called them with the news on Memorial Day, the worst weekend in the year, when summer employees and tourists descend in droves! Shelley had no prior warning when the phone rang. Their landlady summarily announced that she needed their rented home in Wilson for a new employee. There was no other affordable housing for him available.

"'Then what are *we* supposed to do?' I asked her," Shelley shouted over the canned music and cacophony of Saturday night voices.

"You know the area. I'm sure you'll find something," the woman said. "Be out in thirty days."

The Rubrechts had to move into a small apartment in town while they tried to find another house.

The Rubrecht team has been a Jackson institution for two decades. Shelley's old-fashioned fiddling and Kelly's lead guitar have kept heels stomping in "the Hole" into the wee hours of many a night in local bistros and at civic functions. During the day, Kelly tests water quality for the city. Shelley teaches violin lessons and waitresses at Anthony's Restaurant. They thought they had planted roots. Now Kelly's not so sure.

"We're have-nots here," he said. "We've been here twenty years and still don't own a piece of property. The only places to buy are Cottonwood Park and Rafter J. Rafter J lots are $45,000. In Cottonwood Park you could still get one for $38,000. Lots barely on the edge of town go up to $150,000. What amuses me is realtors putting in an ad saying, 'Here's the perfect starter home for the fixer-upper—$137,000.' What happens is the people that are our friends are being driven out of the community. And we may be, too, because we can't afford to live here."

But it was the high-end residential developments–Teton Village, Teton Pines, John Dodge, the Jackson Hole Racquet Club, Spring Creek Ranch, Jackson Hole Golf and Tennis Estates–that made the big difference. Gone were the authentic log cabins furnished with leather sofas and Navajo rugs that the early millionaires built. Instead, the valley swelled with 6,000 to 12,000-square-foot customized homes in contemporary, traditional, or colonial styles that could fit into almost any neighborhood in the country. There were guest houses, hot tubs, exercise rooms, offices fitted with fax machines and high-tech computers. Million-dollar price tags became commonplace. Second-home status was prevalent.

"Desanctification by bulldozer for bucks," Jack Huyler calls it.

Explosive growth introduced new people who brought their own values. They came from Miami, Beverly Hills, even Tokyo. Enjoying their posh vacation hideaways only a few weeks of the year and used to living in high-crime urban areas, they didn't feel comfortable without twenty-four hour security and property management. The resulting walled enclaves and massive berms surrounding exclusive developments precluded neighborliness.

Rod and Chris Eastman still feel burned over their venture into the Teton Pines resort community about ten miles west of town.

The Eastmans were out for an evening drive. Chris, a real estate agent and third-generation Jackson Holer, was familiar with most properties for sale in the county but hadn't had a chance to check what was currently happening at Teton Pines. Rod suggested a spin through the back section.

Their antiquated Chevrolet Suburban pulled off the Moose-Wilson Road and crossed the bridge over a small lake that fed water through a championship Arnold Palmer golf course stretching to the south. They wound along the driveway past the clubhouse, an elegant contemporary structure of grayed wood with vaulted ceilings and walls of windows overlooking groves of aspen and pine and a lush putting green in the shadow of the Teton Mountains. North of the club was a landscaped swimming pool. Across from a spacious parking lot stood a John Gardiner tennis complex with a large indoor pavilion and a dozen outdoor hard courts. Beyond lay a polo field and acres of woods where million-dollar estates and cluster homes boasting marble floors, multiple fireplaces, and lavish entertainment centers were beginning to appear.

When they reached the intersection of Clubhouse and Teton Pines drives, a uniformed guard stopped them at a new gatehouse that had been erected at the entrance to the residential section.

"Excuse me," he said, eying their beat-up car. "Do you live here?"

"No."

"Are you visiting a resident?"

"No."

"I'm sorry, the gate is closed. Nobody but owners and registered guests are allowed to enter."

"He didn't even allow us to pull through the gate and turn around in the driveway," Chris says.

The Eastmans had never been denied entry in Jackson Hole.

"It was my first indication that Jackson was developing a class system of the rich and those who are not worthy," she says. "We have always had wealthy people, but you never could tell who they were. We could always drive by their homes. We don't trespass on people's property."

Jack Huyler agrees. "You didn't use to be able to tell who was the wealthy rancher," he says. "And the waitress in the restaurant might have well been the daughter of that wealthy rancher. It was a class-less society."

"Jackson is known as an open, friendly type of community and people who were already here resent the security," says Dave Spackman, a partner in Teton Pines. "[But] a lot of people here come from places like Los Angeles, Miami, and New York and they're just not comfortable without it."

Many residents blame the part-time population for triggering other changes in Jackson's traditional lifestyle.

"With second-home people it's not their town," says Mickey Waller. "They're not interested in who's on the school board and whether eighty-five-year-old Mrs. McGillicuty fell down and broke her leg and somebody ought to take her something to eat. That whole feeling of community, *esprit de corps*, loving your neighbor is something that Jackson always had. If I broke down on the road at night I didn't have to worry about who stopped to help me or that someone wouldn't stop to help me. They would. That whole feeling is gone in Jackson."

Suddenly the people who migrated to Jackson for its wild scenery, outdoor recreation and frontier flavor started clamoring for paved roads, airport expansion for jet service and increased cultural facilities. Instead of fitting into frontier life themselves, they tried to impose upon their new home the gentrification of the places they had left. Polarization of the community resulted.

"One big change is in the manner of fund-raising," says Nancy Hoffman, who came to fish in 1978 and stayed to marry lifetime resident Gene Hoffman.

"Over the years the hospital auxiliary has had a 'Spring Fling' at Jackson Lake Lodge. They'd tap the community for those who believe in that particular cause and ask for a $25 contribution. The meal and band were donated. Every year they would have about 350 people. You'd see everything from blue jeans to ballroom gowns. And nobody cared. It's now the major donors. You go for the big dollars. You wouldn't think of wearing anything but a gown that represented something very expensive to compete with another gal."

Jack Huyler refuses to conform. He won't wear a tie, much less a tuxedo.

"The worst I ever got was an invitation in French to come to a fancy party at a chateau," he says. "What the hell is Jackson Hole going to come to? Most people came here to get away from that. What gets me is that people escape from California—from something they dislike—and then they mold the place they've come to in that image. And they all have a dreadful similarity."

Yet a few people are able to retain vestiges of the "real" Jackson Hole. Bob and Claire McConaughy, managers of Howard Stirn's R Lazy S Ranch, operate one of the handful of surviving guest ranches in the county. Comfortably garbed in well-worn boots, jeans, leather vests and ten-gallon Stetsons, they haven't changed their method of dude wrangling since they took over the McConaughy family spread in a different location in 1954. The ranch boasts individual log cabins, a roomy main lodge with a rock fireplace, rough-hewn pine furniture, a fine collection of western art and "three squares a day," suited to appetites galvanized by lots of clean, fresh air. Activities center around a stable of horses and the magnificent Tetons that tower over the valley.

"A lot of dude ranches have turned into resorts with swimming pools and all," says Claire. "But we've tried very hard not to do that. The atmosphere is the same. The attitudes."

"The chamber of commerce and other people in town are trying very hard to retain the western flavor and justify its claim of Jackson as the real West," says Bob. "But it's probably a little far-fetched at this point to call it the last of the Old West. The major issue now is how much growth can the valley take and do the people want. And what should we do about that?"

four: LITTLE TOWN BLUES

"If you want to do something real Santa Fe-ish, get a Fritos Pie at Woolworth's. Then eat it on the Plaza. Very traditional," says Suzanne Hubner.

The city manager sits at a conference table centering her spacious contemporary office in city hall. A block to the south, Native Americans squat beneath the portal of the Palace of the Governors on the historic Plaza. Handcrafted turquoise-and-silver jewelry is spread before them on blankets. Pods of tourists, hanging with cameras, backpacks, and plastic shopping bags logoed by Beneton, the Plaza Poster Gallery, and the Santa Fe T-Shirt Co., haggle for bargains.

"Woolworth's is the only store left for locals to shop in," Hubner says somewhat wistfully. "About five years ago Kahn's Shoe Store closed on the Plaza. That to me was symbolic, a real change. And they [merchants] have gone quickly."

With Southwest-ism almost a national cult drawing hordes of visitors every year, it has become increasingly difficult to maintain the city's time-honored ambiance. The desire to cater to tourists wanting souvenirs of their visit to "The City Different" has wrought many changes.

"There's a real battle between retaining the Santa Fe that people want to come to see with the number of people coming to see it who are in and of themselves changing what they want to see," Hubner says.

The council and mayor stood their ground on a request for the touristy horse-drawn carriages that clomp along the streets of many cities.

"Santa Fe never had them and we don't want them," Hubner

says. But around the town square, where an obelisk marks the end of the fabled Santa Fe Trail, local merchants found there was more demand for cheap, wooden pink and green coyotes than for dry goods and household hardware. Residents, impatient with lengthy waits to dodge traffic while crossing the street, fled to suburban shopping malls, where there was ample parking and they could purchase necessities. Property owners, bent on receiving the highest possible return for their investments in the limited downtown space, raised rents until their former tenants could not meet the overhead and high-end boutiques and art galleries replaced them.

Santa Feans decry disregard in recent years of their architectural standards of scale and Spanish Colonial style that have given their community its special identity.

"The First Interstate Bank was a turning point as far as bigger structures," Hubner says. "Even though it got through the Historic District review, it's massive. The big controversy was the Eldorado Hotel. The local people don't like it because it just isn't 'Santa Fe.'" Some say the over sized, box-shaped hotel, which was constructed in 1985 on the site of a much-beloved hardware store, looks like a prison.

In a 1990 pre-city-election poll, 64.8 percent of those questioned accused government officials of excessive leniency with real estate developers.

"Over a period of time the downtown has been pretty much given away to tourism," says Debbie Jaramillo, city councilwoman since 1988 and a close contender with incumbent mayor Sam Pick in 1990. "The local people felt they just didn't belong. Santa Fe has been sold to the highest bidder, and they're going to be standing in line to collect for years."

Scenarios similar to those in Santa Fe can be found in Jackson, Aspen, Park City, Sun Valley, and other places throughout the West. As a town is taken over by tourism and more people move in, the population becomes layered and polarized. The old-timers, those who were born there or have lived most of their lives in the area, are most affected by changes as their town achieves success as a resort. They are torn between two realities. They remember former days when mining or ranching thrived, when the population was small and homogeneous and everyone knew his neighbor. Their memories hold pictures of a life that was even and uncomplicated, that moved at a stroll rather than a sprint.

They also remember the bad times when the economy virtually collapsed under depressed prices for ore or beef and escalating costs of production. The young people, seeing no future for themselves, moved away and left a few old-timers with boarded-up Main Streets and weed-covered schoolyards.

In many towns city fathers promised that turning to tourism would improve the flagging economy. Most people went along with the idea. Many figured it was just a stopgap until the ranching or mining industries they preferred were able to make a comeback. They were amused and hospitable as tourists flocked into their rustic towns to recreate, browse, absorb the culture—and leave.

But then the visitors started to stay. Hippies and city folk moved in permanently. Old-timers became resentful because they felt that new lifestyles that they didn't want, need, or respect were being foisted on them. The fancy clothes, French bistros, and health-food markets seemed out of place and supplanted the stores and restaurants they needed, enjoyed, and could afford. Many who had lived in these communities all their lives pulled up stakes.

Art Durante was one of the last holdouts in Park City. His rickety wooden hardware store was a fixture on Main Street for years. Customers could go in and rummage through the chaos of ratchets, dishpans, copper tubing and snow shovels and find most anything they needed. Art always barked out a snappy insult and everyone loved it. But finally, as decrepit buildings in Old Town got facelifts or gave way to modern brick structures housing elite furriers, art galleries, fancy sportswear stores, and import shops, Art's falling-down store was deemed obsolete and an eyesore. And a valuable piece of property. Art, tantalized by a hefty price he couldn't resist, sold his business and moved to Las Vegas.

Skyrocketing real estate values changed the lives of homeowners, too. Parkites Tom and Emily Sullivan had added a wing to their modest house a block away from the Park City Ski Area. Lifelong residents of the town, they considered themselves comfortably settled for their "golden years." But one day the historic Miner's Hospital across the street was jacked onto a flatbed truck and moved to City Park to become the library. A massive condominium complex started to rise in its place. Developers then hammered on the Sullivan's door with offers to buy their property. They didn't want to sell; they loved their home and wanted to remain near friends and family. But pretty soon the offering price became so tempting that they couldn't refuse. They bought another place down canyon in Salt Lake City and their old house was moved to a new development in the county to make room for another condominium.

While many old-timers in all these communities have pulled up roots and left, a few have remained, resigned to changing conditions. They get together at senior centers and reminisce about old times.

Howard Walters, a "retired but unretired" carpenter in Jackson Hole, feels somewhat displaced. He is digging into a plateful of fried chicken, mashed potatoes and gravy, and corn on the cob at the Don McLeod Center when I meet him. The dining room in the brown frame building is noisy with jocular cotton-haired women in pantsuits and men with weather-tested faces seated at long tables along both sides of the room. Photographs and paintings of familiar local scenes hang on the walls.

"What was Jackson like when you were a kid?" I ask Walters.

"It was a pretty nice place. I lived right uptown." he answers.

"How big was your school?"

"The high school was 125 students. Now they have more than that in one class."

"What do you think of the growth?"

"My favorite expression is we've had a lot of growth, a lot of changes, and dang little improvement."

Thelma, across the table, nods in agreement. "It's very uncom-fortable to go to town. You never see anyone you know. It's strange."

"Has development helped the economy?" I ask Walters.

"Well, I suppose it has," he answers. "It's raised our taxes."

"What are some of the things you like about the town?"

Howard puts down his fork and looks up for the first time.

"The bad part is I don't know any different," he says, thoughtful-ly. "I don't know how it would be to live anywhere else."

Although long-time residents of expanding communities throughout the West have had to deal with the difficulties attendant with changing and growing populations, there have been some bene-fits. Low-paying resort jobs are better than no jobs at all. Those with school-age children are reaping the rewards of improved educational systems that make college a possibility not previously considered. Activities and meals for senior citizens, modern grocery stores, and expanded city services are welcome additions. The disadvantage of higher property taxes is counteracted by the increased value of land or buildings. Their biggest complaints, other than the cost of living and crowded conditions, concern the changed, unfamiliar appear-ance of their hometowns and the imposition of different values.

Long-term Santa Fe residents—both Anglo and Hispanic—feel pushed aside by the "wealthy outsider [who] moves here and puts up his electronic gates to keep people out," says Debbie Jaramillo.

Hispanics, in particular, feel that their traditional culture, which has predominated in the state for four hundred years, is threatened.

"People move here and they bring their values with them," the city councilwoman continues. "What they came here for, supposedly, was the clean air, environment, mellowness of the town. But before we knew it, they needed their expensive restaurants, boutiques, nightlife, and so-called culture. Well, some people can't afford their symphonies and operas. And we're not interested in some of it because our cultural background is tied to the Spanish. We have lost our language. We have been forced to assimilate another culture instead of them coming here and assimilating into our dominant culture. And once the trade is made, you can't go back."

Native Americans in Sedona resent New Agers who are imitating their rituals and customs. They don't want their sacred mountains desecrated by false medicine wheels and other sacramental signs.

"The New Agers are pseudo-Indians exploiting our culture," says Reuben Snake, director of the Native American Religious Freedom Project, whose supporters argue that the land should be kept the way their ancestors left it.

Long-time residents in most of these resorts are uncomfortable with the reputation their towns have acquired as frivolous places where there are more bibs and parkas than overalls, where men with ponytails and earrings are as plentiful as cowboys once were, and where weekend bikers compete with pickup trucks for space on two-lane country roads.

"I call Jackson Hole the great national playpen," says Virginia Huidekoper. "Nora's Cafe, down in Wilson, has three tiers of social life in the morning. Before eight o'clock, it's the guys that are working and you find out what's being built and what's going on. Then they leave. Between eight and nine are the independent, self-employed group, like architects, artists, etc. Then at nine comes the play set. So the parking lot starts out with pickup trucks, then changes to ordinary cars, and at nine o'clock everything that comes in has a rack on top with surfboards, bicycles, or some kind of play device."

One might say rural towns that have become resorts are reminiscent of the elephant and the blind men. Everyone has a personal view of the place. Each reacts to the towering mountain peaks, the surrealistic desert, or the quaint village but is there for different reasons.

Some of the locals—a generally accepted term for people who have lived there fifteen years or more—came initially as developers or seasonal employees when a ski area or other recreational complex was created. Others discovered the community as tourists. In most cases it was love at first sight that caused them to stay or return as permanent residents. These persons became the first wave of rebuilders who fixed up historic buildings and started small businesses; constructed condominiums, hotels, and recreational facilities to accommodate visitors; volunteered on community projects; and held public office. Their efforts gave the crumbling towns a facelift and a revived personality.

More recent newcomers have arrived as the resorts' reputations have waxed. A mixed group with divergent values, many are retirees or escapees from big-city pollution and congestion who have been drawn by the scenic natural settings and recreational opportunities in these resort communities. They consider live theatre, arts centers, concerts, and fine restaurants extra bonuses. Knowing they can live anywhere and still connect with clients in their former metropolises via electronics, they replace hours of commuting with time spent enjoying their new paradise. Once settled, they would just as soon close the door on any more like themselves.

Then come the more recent developers who are eager to take advantage of financial opportunities and plunge into real estate or land development once the resort has acquired a favorable reputation. Since the main part of town is usually built up by the time they arrive, they have no choice but to build further from the town's center. They construct subdivisions and elaborate condos in styles that they think are reminiscent of world-class resorts—and they are sure their efforts will enhance the attractiveness of the town. They also introduce large shopping malls with fast-food franchises, discount stores, and factory outlets.

Finally come the activists—people dedicated to "cleaning up the town." They work to rid city council of those who would bring back extractive industries or allow a monopoly of real estate professionals to urbanize the area and despoil the surrounding environment.

As chambers of commerce proselytize and resorts expand, certain resorts are deemed fashionable by the rich and famous. The celebrities make brief retreats to their vacation homes where they can enjoy reasonable anonymity and wander Main Street without being bothered. Many of them, like actor Harrison Ford of Jackson Hole, contribute to the preservation of the natural environment by dedicating a portion of their immense holdings to the Nature Conservancy or by creating land trusts that remain undeveloped for posterity.

But sometimes when the presence of such notables is used in promotion of the area, the publicity backfires. When television star Dennis Weaver selected Ridgway, Colorado, as the site of his ranch, he never dreamed his public enthusiasm for the place would come back to haunt him. Weaver attracted national attention to the area when he built a widely publicized, environmentally conscious home that incorporated, among other materials, recycled automobile tires.

Situated on U.S. Highway 550 midway between Durango and Grand Junction, the small village of Ridgway sits in open rangeland with a staggering view of the saw-toothed San Juan peaks. The town, which was the setting for the John Wayne movie *True Grit*, is a cross-roads between Telluride, in the mountains to the west, Ouray, a restored Victorian mining camp and hot springs resort a few miles south, and the regional commercial center of Montrose to the north. There are a few ranches spread through the broad valley and some historic buildings bordering a tiny town square. The county rodeo grounds gather dust until they come alive with Professional Rodeo Association action every Labor Day.

Ridgway remained an unknown pass-through point until 1989, when the Ridgway Reservoir State Park fifteen miles away opened. Suddenly, the area turned into a destination spot where campers and RV owners could enjoy water sports, a full-service marina, campsites providing electric hookups, showers, and flush toilets in a dense juniper forest along the shoreline.

Creation of the recreational attraction prompted the Cim Juan Realty Corporation to commence construction of Ridgway, U.S.A., a commercial/residential development, and "Trail Town" theme park at the juncture of State Highway 62 and U.S. 550. When Cim Juan asked Weaver to film some television commercials for them, he complied. Then in October 1990, just as Ridgway was about to follow the state of Colorado's edict for towns to make a ten-year reassessment of their master plan, a miniature uprising occurred.

The morning before the annual Arts and Crafts Fair, Chris Hollenbeck, a contractor, and Jerry Roberts, a window washer and chimney sweep—a couple of city transplants from the sixties era— became upset over rumors of annexing the Cim Juan acreage into the city to avoid more stringent county jurisdictions. They were horrified at the prospect of outside entrepreneurs triggering growth similar to Telluride's in their town.

"Once the corridor between Ridgway and Ouray is destroyed, it's all over," Hollenbeck said. "A place like this should have a dues-paying club. It's not for everyone. It should choose the people, not the people with dollars choose to come in and buy it up. There's a core of people who think the place is worth saving. It's not something God gave us to pave."

Hollenbeck and Roberts also objected to the fact that Weaver had been making videos and advertisements for Ridgway, U.S.A., selling the area as the last unspoiled region in Colorado. They interpreted Weaver's involvement as that of a newcomer from Hollywood coming in and selling off the place. So before daylight the day of the festival, they rallied some friends and plastered the town with about two hundred posters of Weaver's likeness in a circle with a slash through it.

The town fathers were furious. They ordered the marshal to tear down the offending posters.

But it was too late. Everyone in town had seen them.

Dennis Weaver was upset. And crushed. He had no intention of hurting his adopted community, he protested.

"The locals explained that they simply felt he provided the focus for a growing debate over the appropriateness of rapid growth in the Ridgway area," Art Goodtimes later wrote in *The Telluride Times-Journal*.

The national media is full of stories about movie stars and

jet-setters escaping to the small-town West. More and more wealthy second-homers follow in their footsteps to build elegant condos and homes in the high seven figures that are used a few weeks of the year. With them come the glitz of mink-lined parkas and restaurants serving $800 bottles of wine and pheasant-under-glass.

Once the population diversifies, it is only natural that polarization occurs between the wealthy, the working class, and various ethnic groups.

In Jackson, social stratification has even reached the schoolroom. When Virginia Huidekoper's youngsters attended the Wilson School, there were thirty-five students, three rooms, and eight grades. You couldn't tell who was the woodcutter's daughter or the budding heiress. Nowadays, there are 130 pupils for five grades, and many of the kids are picked up after class by nannies driving Mercedes.

As the monied set rolls in, ranchers and farmers are tantalized by offers for spreads that have been in the family for generations. Many resorts are surrounded by public lands—national and state parks, U.S. Forest and BLM property. Consequently, the miniscule amount of private land becomes prized. Irrigated land that once sold for $34.58 an acre brings $25–30,000 up to several hundred thousand. Price appears to be no object to the buyers. Developers negotiate huge bank loans to buy up agricultural acreage and build golf courses, huge discount stores, or gated residential complexes. Besides shrinking the limited and precious open space, profits often go to big corporations or entrepreneurs from outside of the area who have come to snap up ground-floor bargains.

With recreation replacing the closed-down mines or flagging agricultural economy as the dominant industry, locals are subject to low-paying jobs that are service-oriented. As thankful as they are that tourism has brought their town out of depression, their cost of living has escalated and it is difficult to adjust to wages far below the $35,000 they earned blasting ore.

"Heber people loved working in the [Park City, Utah] mines," says Bob Mathis, Wasatch County planner. "Those were big wages and a very manful job. They could support their families and subsidize their farms. Their wives didn't have to work. They'd be buying new cars, fixing their houses, and riding their horses—all of those things that make up the psyche of the western man.

"Now, the wife's got to work and they have to adjust to jobs they wouldn't ordinarily have considered. That's because they're uneducated."

Other service employees, who were attracted to the area by the recreational activities and action-packed lifestyle, can't afford the high cost of living in town anymore. The irony is that they are needed to operate the chairlifts, mow the golf course fairways, serve the racks of lamb, pour the martinis, and scour the bathrooms. But commuting isn't easy.

Vickie Shephard, of Midway, Utah, crawls out of bed before daylight on snowy winter mornings and has to turn on the porch light to see if the Wasatch County plows have reached her neighborhood yet. When it's hard to tell where the yard stops and the road begins she knows she'll have to get an early start. There's Jimmy and Justin to roust out of bed in time to bolt down some breakfast and catch the elementary school bus. She'll have to give them instructions on how to microwave their dinner as she won't be home until after 9:00 P.M. About 8:00 A.M. she'll coax her brown 1983 Eagle through the snowdrifts to Highway 40 and the twenty-five-mile drive to Park City. She'll spend the next thirteen hours hauling her vacuum and cleaning equipment to the condominiums and homes she maintains.

Vickie makes $15 an hour. She cleans ten condos and an equal number of private homes during the high season. But it slows down in summer. As a single parent, however, she cannot afford living in the town where she works, much as she'd like to.

Jenny Smith, of the employee services department at the Park City Ski Area, estimates that about forty percent of the resort's employees commute from neighboring towns such as Oakley, Coalville, Kamas, Heber City, and Midway. She and her contractor husband, Eric, are among them.

Affordable housing is a problem in all western resort towns.

The classified section in an October 1990 *Aspen Times* listed a studio apartment in the Colorado resort for $740 a month. A three-bedroom, three-bath home rented for $5,500. A 360-square-foot remodeled hotel room with a refrigerator and microwave was advertised for $475. The few low-income apartments and condos had as many as sixty-five potential renters signed up for units upon availability. One property manager finally threw away the waiting list that had become "a clerical nightmare." Consequently, many blue-collars squeeze into ghettolike trailer parks a few miles from city center. Scores of waitresses, bartenders, carpenters, and snowcat operators drive back and forth on the narrow, mountainous "Killer 82" to Carbondale, Basalt, Cardiff, or Glenwood Springs.

The dangers and hardships of a commuting work force aren't the only problems. Shuttling employees lack identification with either community. They spend most of their time where they collect their paycheck, yet they don't vote, pay taxes, or send their kids to school there. There is no feeling of belonging, no sense of commitment.

"A regrettable thing is we've lost a bit of the tapestry of the town because of the high prices forcing [employees] out and pressing them down valley," says Aspen's former mayor, Bill Stirling. "Some locals moved down valley because they knew they never could get a corner here. In order to get a sufficient amount of land or a place to raise a family, they decided that the commute would be worth it. In the last eighteen years, we've lost about thirty percent of the workers who have moved down valley or out of the valley altogether."

Already Jackson Hole employees obliged to live in Idaho are getting fed up with the daily commute across the Tetons.

Mickey Waller says, "This fall I went to a filling station and the same little kid that has pumped my gas and worked on my car for four or five years said, 'Well, better tell you goodbye, Mickey. My wife says she won't spend another winter driving around that pass. We're leaving.'"

Jackson is losing middle-income people as well. Couples who hold managerial positions and can well afford to buy a home around $125,000 are leaving the area because there is nothing available at that price that they would consider living in.

Even mobile home courts are scarce—and often denigrated.

"To the people of ultra wealth saying you live in a mobile home court is like saying, 'I have the clap, would you like to kiss me?'" says Waller, who lives in the largest park several miles south of town. "They think it's terrible. Yet where are these working people going to live?"

Kelly Rubrecht fears the population will become one-sided.

"What worries me about Jackson ten or twenty years from now is it's going to be economically homogeneous. Everybody the same," he says.

Environmental author Jon Bowermaster claims Aspen locals are even "scared that the town will soon become the exclusive hangout for the fabulously rich and that their end of the valley may be nothing but an opulent ghost town during much of the year, with the million-dollar second homes shuttered, the streets quiet and lifeless."

Concerned citizens throughout the entire western region are demanding that their city councils provide affordable housing in order to stem the exodus of a working class. Public outcry prompted Aspen's housing authority to shell out over $2 million to purchase three in-town parcels. Councilman Frank Peters justified the expense in order "to maintain Aspen's community character by ensuring that at least some of the homeowners in town are people who work here and live here full-time."

The reality of affordable housing in other towns is slow in coming, however. There are plans and a great deal of talk in Telluride, Park City, and other resorts; but red tape in matters of funding and waiving of city building fees and permits imposes delays. Meanwhile, a secondary impact is taking place in nearby communities.

While resorts are getting top-heavy with millionaires, the

neighboring villages are starting to see more than lower-paid employees moving down valley. Little farming towns are filling up with those disillusioned by the commercialization of the "undiscovered" places they originally escaped to fifteen or twenty years before.

Mike Warner, Hailey, Idaho's, first full-time city planner, attributes his small town's amazing seventy-four-percent leap in population during the past ten years to the influx of people leaving nearby Sun Valley. Not wanting to depart the area entirely but weary of the runaway growth, they sell their property for a good profit and move south to a more bucolic environment. There they can assemble a pre-manufactured home on a larger and less expensive site for approximately $45–50 a square foot. Contrast that to the valley, where an average home is 1,900 square feet at about $210 per square foot. And nowadays, there aren't very many average homes—most are a good deal larger.

When Gary and Shelley Weiss moved to Park City to operate Dolly's Bookstore with his parents, Norm and Clair Weiss, the resort town was too citified for them. They had had it with suburban living in New York, Phoenix, Denver, and southern California. It was the rural life they were after. So they chose Oakley, a hamlet of about 525 residents nestled at the foot of the Uinta Mountains. There, with two acres of land, four horses, and five dogs, they have their bit of paradise.

"The town is remote enough that there is not a lot of development," Gary says. "No sewer. No natural gas. No doctor. No cable television, and the nearest supermarket is in Park City, twenty-five miles away. For us, that's an advantage because it's a disincentive for people to move here."

Weiss considers the dearth of water a mixed blessing. While he sees the town fathers starting to take an interest in planning, he hopes that the probability of much speculative development is negligible.

As outsiders, the Weisses have different priorities from the locals, many of whom have family roots spanning over a hundred years. Not of the predominant Mormon faith, environmentalists and

Downtown Aspen.

New replaces old town, Aspen.

Security housing, a new western trend?

Chuckwagon breakfast, keeping tradition alive.

The Heritage House, a preservation of history, Kanab, Utah.

Ranger at Newspaper Rock, near Moab, Utah.

Old Miners Hospital, now the library in Park City.

Telltale storefront, Aspen.

vegetarians as well, they still live comfortably and are accepted in the tight-knit community of ranchers because they don't attempt to force their ways on long-time residents. Gary even has the honor of announcing the Fourth of July parade preceding Oakley's biggest event, the annual rodeo.

Integration of newcomers into little communities with an ingrown population isn't always so easy. In 1980 Art Goodtimes, who had lived on both coasts, came to Colorado for a job with the Telluride Film Festival. A tortuous drive along the San Miguel River took him high into the Uncompahgre National Forest where the road dead-ended in a box canyon cloistered by jagged thirteen-thousand-foot peaks. It was irresistible to Goodtimes. He decided to stay.

Telluride was in the process of shedding its mining image and becoming a major western winter resort. In the late sixties a Beverly Hills lawyer and entrepreneur named Joe Zoline envisioned a ski area in what was then a ghost town. He purchased land and commenced construction on a resort that he boasted would be "bigger than Vail, as large as Ajax, Aspen Highlands, and Buttermilk combined, and twice as big as Mammoth in California."

When Goodtimes arrived, the metamorphosis was already underway. Real estate prices had skyrocketed and there was nothing within his reach. He moved forty miles down valley to Norwood.

Norwood is a conservative ranching community of approximately four hundred residents, most of whom have lived there all their lives. Change comes slowly there; locals are comfortable with the status quo. They resent their town being identified as a bedroom community of Telluride. They're not quite sure what they think of newcomers.

Goodtimes, heavily bearded and scraggly-haired, looks a bit out of place as he breakfasts at Karen's Cafe on Main Street. There's a sixsome of hunters wearing orange caps in the back corner. The drop-ins' table by the window is filling up with cowboys gathering for their daily scuttlebutt session. Karen is feverishly dishing out home-style flapjacks, hash-brown potatoes, and ham and eggs from the kitchen pass-through in the rear.

"There's a wide gap between people who live here," Goodtimes says. "Not in income so much, but in lifestyle. I've been here ten years and I'm just now starting to feel sort of accepted. I don't feel odd walking into the post office anymore."

Population increases in rural communities create other, negative impacts. While city services and the educational systems of the Park Citys, Aspens, and Jackson Holes benefit from property taxes on exorbitant real estate, the Oakleys, Carbondales, and Driggses suffer from greater demands on more modest financial bases.

"You can't have the growth without more kids in the schools, more demand on water and sewer systems, and the tax base does not always appear where the services are needed," says R. Thayne Robson, director of the University of Utah Bureau of Economic and Business Research.

"Communities will get increases in demands for services before they get any real expansion in their tax base if they're serving a booming community nearby. The issue is the lag time between when people start to come and load the services prior to the time that the spending patterns they generate both increase tax revenues and make viable other types of commercial enterprises."

Idaho communities on the back side of the Tetons from Jackson Hole are in that time lag. The towns of Driggs and Victor are filling with commuters from the resort, most of whom are on the lower end of the wage scale. Homes that have been on the market for years are sold out. Trailer courts are converging on the south end of Teton Valley. Schools are so full that temporary classrooms are in use and there is talk of a bond issue to build a new high school.

Yet Driggs has not caught up with the growth. The town has lost its automobile dealer, farm implement store, and a couple of small groceries. Victor, in the south valley, doesn't even have a supermarket. And farmers, who have harvested crops for generations, are struggling to stay in business as land is being chopped up for mobile home parks and small horse farms.

"The Jackson Hole commuters draw their pay in Wyoming and

do most of their buying on that side of the mountain," says Mike Whitfield, a lifelong resident of the little agricultural community. "But they depend on our schools and services."

Child care is another issue facing the bedroom towns. As resort personnel move in, there is a need for day-care centers and after-school youth programs. Older children often experience behavioral problems when there is no one home to oversee them. The *Denver Post* reported that case loads of social workers in Pitkin and Garfield counties near Aspen have escalated, and calls about child abuse and neglect are common.

But there are still many rural communities who would settle for such growing pains in return for a boost to their stagnant economies. Towns that haven't experienced a growth spurt are in the same position the resorts were twenty or thirty years ago and they are envious.

The October 22, 1990, *Southern Utah News* bemoaned that "Kanab, like many other Utah towns, has become merely a stopover as weary travelers head 'someplace else.'"

Residents of Kanab, in "Utah's Color Country," can't understand why Moab and St. George are taking off and they aren't. They, too, are surrounded by redrock cliffs. They are a stone's throw away from national parks and recreational areas like Glen Canyon Dam, Lake Powell, the Grand Canyon, Zion National Park and Bryce Canyon. They have the nine-hole Coral Cliff Golf Course, dune buggying on the Coral Pink Sand Dunes, a couple of modern motels, and the historic Parry Lodge, where rooms are named for Jimmy Stewart, Frank Sinatra, John Wayne, and other stars who once slept there.

But the movie companies have long forgotten the place they once called "Little Hollywood." Environmental opposition has curtailed the once-profitable logging industry. Tourists usually stop just long enough to fill up the gas tank, pick up a forgotten loaf of bread, or buy a souvenir "picture rock."

Perhaps Kanabites don't realize how fortunate they are. Their uncrowded town is virtually untouched. The restored Queen Anne-style Heritage House presides over Main Street. Pioneer homes sit in the shade of Lombardy poplars and mock orange trees. Store windows display authentic western wear and Indian arts and crafts. The eclectic Artistic Design Kanab Floral and Ceramic Shop boasts two-day film development, flowers, ceramics, greenware, classes, kiln, wedding announcements, and tuxedo rental—all under one roof. There are a few real estate companies pushing sales of Kanab Creek Ranchos, Cedar Heights Estates, and town homes overlooking the golf course, but tabs run far below the $100,000 and $1 million mark of the established resorts.

On the other end of the spectrum is Bullhead City, Arizona.

Once known as Hardyville, the pioneer Colorado River steamboat port disappeared with the frontier. Then Davis Dam was built by the Bureau of Reclamation in the 1950s and a big rock shaped like a bull's head was flooded by the newly created Mohave Lake. A handful of river people, government workers, and retirees stayed on to fish and camp and the little village was reborn. They named it Bullhead City.

Homer Fancher, the former postmaster, is a lifelong resident. He's watched it burgeon from a few houses, Nick Law's Bait Shop, Bert Williams' boat dock, a grocery store, and a couple of bars into one of Arizona's fastest-growing communities, with 10,364 residents in 1980 and 21,287 in 1990. Sitting on the front porch of his home overlooking the river, he remembers how it used to be.

"When I was a kid, down on the river bottom there was only one road in," he says. "The Cotton Land Company had cotton farms down there in the early days. And hogs."

He points to the Nevada shoreline across the water and shakes his head in amazement. Out of the flat, dun-colored desert tower the Flamingo Hilton, Harrah's, the Golden Nugget, Holiday Inn, the Colorado Belle, the Riverside, and the twenty-six-story Edgewater, each with hundreds of rooms, seafood bars, all-you-can-eat prime rib buffets, convention facilities, lounges with live entertainment, swimming pools and spas, and, of course, the casinos. The sandy beaches nearby fill with bathers, and hotel boat-landing ramps teem with gamblers and bar-hoppers shuttling among the attractions in jet launches, open-sided ferries, and even a Mississippi-style paddle-wheel steamboat.

"There used to be nothing but cliffs coming right down to the water," Fancher says. "You couldn't get down to the river because there were such high banks. They cut those mountains down and moved them out."

It all started in 1966 when Don Laughlin, the thirty-five-year-old proprietor of a North Las Vegas bar, piloted his plane over a drab and dusty strip of desert along the north bank of the Colorado River. Below him was a bankrupt bar with a few slots, a bait shop, and a seedy, eight-room motel. Mohave Lake sparkled downriver. Bullhead City slept on the opposite shore. A perfect place for a gambling mecca, the visionary Laughlin figured—a unique gambling mecca targeting those who coveted, but couldn't afford, the expensive fun in Las Vegas or Reno. The area was already licensed for gaming. It could draw crowds from Arizona, Southern California, and Utah, who could stay and play in bargain-priced hotels, camp in RV parks, and gamble for small stakes. Convinced that his idea would fly, he sold his bar and settled by the river.

Laughlin's unlikely investment turned into "an overnight success twenty-plus years in the making," he laughs. And the 2,500-acre town named for its founder claims over 5,000 residents at last count and is Nevada's fastest-growing resort. Don Laughlin donated $3 million to span a bridge across the water and connect his little kingdom to Arizona. Arizona widened State Highway 95 to put Phoenix four hours away, and Los Angeles is a five-hour drive, and Las Vegas one-and-a-half hours. With nine casinos, a room count of close to 10,000, and parking lots packed with motor homes, gaming revenues rank third in the state.

According to Fancher, both Laughlin and Bullhead City are just on the edge.

"Originally, most of the people moving here were retirees because they could buy a lot and put a trailer on it within their income," he says. "But you haven't seen the growth here you're going to see."

A fifty-passenger Convair taking off from the neighboring Bullhead-Laughlin Airport roars low over Fancher's home.

"We'll be getting 737s when the new runway's completed," he says. "And now that we've got the sewer, they're going to start building [in Bullhead City]. There will be some more motels, quite a few RV parks—and another two or more golf courses are on the books, with homes all around them."

He watches another plane come in for a landing.

"The rattlesnakes are moving away," he says. Then, half-seriously, he adds, "Now we've got snakes in the grass."

While booming Bullhead City's chamber of commerce projects a population approaching 100,000 by the year 2000 and still urges, "Come Grow with Us!" struggling communities like Moab and Kanab are saying the same thing. It's a type of desperation and not knowing when to say "when" that grips these little western towns until the detrimental effects of too much success are felt. Communities on the edge of change must look carefully at the other resort towns that are now singing the runaway-growth blues. It is never too early for a community to decide what it wants to be and then set the wheels in motion to achieve that goal.

five: FIGHTING WORDS

He was paunchy and pushing sixty. A six-shooter was strapped around his thick middle and his battered black Stetson was set on the back of his head to disclose the wispy, uncombed bangs and famously ugly face. The big man stood next to the short white horse named Little Man and grinned sheepishly when he couldn't get his dusty boot up to the stirrup. Commissioner Cliff Hansen and a couple of other Jackson Hole ranchers led the animal over to a tree stump and helped Wallace Beery mount. Then tiny Parthenia Stinnett, Hansen's sister, and the other heavily armed riders bounded into their saddles and started rounding up the cattle.

It could have been a scene out of *The Man from Dakota* or *Viva Villa*. Once securely holding the reins, the legendary movie star ticked his spurs, trotted over to Parthenia and flashed his tough-guy-with-a-heart-of-gold smile. He was borrowing her horse so it was only fitting that she ride up front with him, the gravelly voice said. They were going to show those sons-of-guns feds.

The Jackson Hole conflict against the federal government and John D. Rockefeller had festered for many years—ever since 1926, when the philanthropic millionaire had offered to purchase and present the nation with approximately 114,000 acres in the Teton Valley. Since that time, the National Park and Forest services—as well as numerous special-interest groups—argued over the particulars of who would assume jurisdiction over the lands. Wyoming congressmen, influenced by a strong livestock lobby and conflicting demands from other counties for federal support, opposed the Interior Department's urging to use the Rockefeller donation to extend Grand Teton National Park. Residents of Teton County rebelled against public ownership of land, which would cheat them out of tax revenues.

On November 27, 1942, Rockefeller himself brought the situation to a head. He informed Secretary of the Interior Harold Ickes that unless the government accepted his gift within a year, he would dispose of the land elsewhere.

It was then that an alternative plan secretly formulated by the Rockefeller interests and the Interior Department surfaced. Since a national park could only be designated by an act of Congress and that appeared impossible, they would bypass opponents to the park expansion by invoking the Antiquities Act of 1906 which allowed the President to set aside the land as a national monument without congressional approval. On March 15, 1943, President Franklin D. Roosevelt did so and signed into law an act that Congress would not even consider five years before.

Reaction was immediate. The Jackson Hole *Courier* issued a scathing "Extra" edition of the paper. The governor and Wyoming congressmen expressed shock and indignation. Drawing upon the anger of a nation at war, Senator Edward Robertson deplored "a foul, sneaking Pearl Harbor blow."

On May 2, a pistol-packing posse of irate Jackson Hole cattlemen staged a symbolic cattle drive to protest Roosevelt's arbitrary order. Churning up a cloud of dust, the defiant westerners trailed some five hundred yearlings across the Gros Ventre River and trespassed into the newly established Jackson Hole National Monument. The ranchers made sure that plenty of reporters were present to let the nation know about the president's legal but, in their opinion, high-handed action that would not only interfere with their use of the land, including their time-honored right to drive stock through the valley to summer range, but would also deprive their county of tax monies. Beery, who was leasing a cabin and half-acre by Jackson Lake from the Forest Service, had nothing in common with the ranchers other than a single milk cow that had just died, but he sympathized with the dispossessed cattlemen and went along to generate more publicity. Besides, he needed a shot of press for his fading film career.

Thirty-six years later, the scenario was almost duplicated in Moab, Utah, when citizens staged a similar rebellion over government restrictions on land use. But this time it was four-wheel-drive vehicles and pickups rather than men on horseback, prayers and speeches instead of guns. The county bulldozer flying an American flag replaced a Hollywood celebrity leading 250 members of the Western Association of Land Users (WALU) and the Grand County commissioners into federally closed roads above Negro Bill Canyon.

"It was Ray Tibbetts's [a former Grand County commissioner] idea," says a fellow commissioner Jimmy Walker. "We constructed a big poster with a logo across it, 'Endangered Species,' illustrating all land uses. Oil, gas, mining, grazing, recreation, you name it.

"It all came about because of the Federal Land Policy and Management Act [FLPMA]. We reasoned that we were being treated as second-class states because of the lack of ability for local governments to control their destinies."

The FLPMA of 1976 was enacted to empower the Bureau of Land Management to review land areas of critical environmental concern. The agency was directed to establish regulations for mining, grazing, and road right-of-way and to identify public lands with wilderness characteristics, study them, and make recommendations as to their suitability for inclusion in the National Wilderness Preservation System. A basic interim management policy banning all development was to be in effect until Congress ruled on future procedures. Any mining that was in progress prior to October 21, 1976, could continue, but no new ventures of any kind would be permitted.

The restrictive act singed the nerves of westerners who had always felt it their given right to exploit the land. They were tired of being hassled by environmentalist extremists who were trying to throw a monkey wrench into their dams, power plants, and other job-producing projects.

City and county commissioners, mining speculators, local

businessmen, national politicians, and representatives of huge energy-producing corporations rallied in a Sagebrush Rebellion to combat the lockup of the mountain West. The tempest raged in Utah, Nevada, and other states battling what they considered federal takeover of their lands.

Their methods were not always benign. When filmmaker Robert Redford opposed Southern California Edison's coal-fired Kaiparowits power plant near Escalante Canyon and Capitol Reef National Park, residents of Kanab burned him in effigy. When Moabite Ken Sleight fought a Trans-Escalante highway, his opponents forced his pickup over a cliff. There were several threatening phone calls and even a bomb scare that evacuated a BLM office.

When the WALU and Grand County commissioners learned that approximately two-thirds of southeastern Utah was included in the BLM's first wilderness inventory map pinpointing roadless tracts of five thousand acres or more, they were incensed. Mineral resources in oil, uranium, gas, potash, and coal produced the largest payroll and tax base in the county.

"We are convinced that wilderness designation will...deny us and a majority of the American people the benefits that these lands can produce today and in the future," WALU committee members Dixie Barker, Paul Rattle, and Ray Tibbetts wrote the BLM.

When locals discovered that some existing routes to mines would remain open but many favorite recreational trails would be out of bounds and four-wheel-drive vehicles disallowed, they were further upset. Typically independent westerners, they had always spread a picnic under any tree that was handy and enjoyed the little back-country paths wherever and whenever they pleased. In addition, considering the rugged topography of the backcountry where one must go around deep canyons, high buttes, and other physical features to get from point A to point B, closing any five thousand acres or more would actually block many more miles of land and deny citizens access to adjacent open areas under state or even private ownership.

"We fear that many uninformed congressmen and bureaucrats

underestimate the importance of our system of rough tracks and vehicular trails in the conduct of our personal lives here," the WALU argued.

"So then the word 'road' came into effect," Jimmie Walker remembers. "What is a road? The BLM position quickly came out that a lot of these things the county was calling 'roads' were no more than 'ways.'"

So the WALU set about proving the 'way' into Negro Bill Canyon was really a 'road.' They made their case with a bulldozer.

First of all a Grand County road crew rammed a bulldozer through a road barrier to the 26,000-acre wilderness inventory unit. Then a second 'dozer driven by a miner chewed up 1.25 miles of track across the canyon floor. The BLM issued a cease-and-desist order and replaced the barrier.

Unfazed, the county bulldozer knocked down the barrier again. The BLM countered by stringing a steel cable across the road and filing a lawsuit. Four days later, the cable was cut.

Moab's bulldozer battles concluded on the Fourth of July when WALU members, Grand County commissioners, and a crowd of locals staged another Sagebrush Rebellion. They gathered on the pink sand flats above town where mounds of slickrock rolled across the desert to the snow-topped La Sal Mountains on the horizon. Overlooking the garbage dump, boasted by the chamber of commerce as "the most scenic in the nation," the commissioners indulged in a bit of oratory extolling the importance of their action. Then the head of the county road department cranked up his bulldozer and, followed by flag-waving celebrants, scraped a path into the floor of Negro Bill Canyon.

"We declared our independence from government control," said Ray Tibbetts. "We rallied at City Park with all the people who were interested, and also the news media, and ran up past the dump area, picked out a road that ran through a given wilderness area and said, 'We're going to prove this is a road...and grade it.'"

BLM manager Gene Day, a staunch supporter of FLPMA, was

beside himself. The rebels were convinced he would throw them in jail. But Washington intervened.

"Gene Day was our biggest obstacle," recalls Jimmie Walker. "He was going to have the federal marshals come in and take us to jail. But we had [Utah Senator] Orrin Hatch back in Washington, keeping an eye on it, to make sure they weren't going to mess with our constitutional rights."

Ultimately, with Hatch's backing, the rebels prevailed. In November 1980, the BLM's final inventory was announced. Negro Bill Canyon and another 1.25 million pristine acres had been dropped from the Moab District's wilderness inventory. Out of 229 roadless areas, 200 had been eliminated. And district manager Gene Day was relieved of his post.

"It was just a matter of time until Gene Day went down the road," quipped Jimmie Walker.

Rebellion against federal authority is a western ethic. The practice thrives to this day. Land. Water. Freedom. These are big words in the West. Fighting words. With so much of the country regulated and restricted, civilian uprisings are common when agencies make unfamiliar changes or revoke traditional rights. Westerners adhere to a live-and-let-live philosophy and figure if it's always been that way that's the way it should stay. Like the annual Moab Jeep Safari during Easter week.

The Red Rock Four-Wheelers blew a gasket in 1990 when it was rumored that the BLM might close some long-used trails and raise fees for their twenty-fifth event the following year. The backcountry junket had been going on since the first few vehicles rumbled through the redrock in 1966. Now there were twelve hundred jeepsters, and gossips broadcast that the long-standing weekly permit fee of .65¢ per vehicle would jump to $1.50 per person per day.

The reports gained credibility when the BLM announced it was preparing a new five-year permit for the group. The event had grown in a single decade from four hundred participants to twelve hundred. There were now twenty-seven trails, instead of ten. Categorical exclusion from the National Environmental Protection Act, which the Safari had always enjoyed under the label of a commercial event, would be withdrawn as events involving fifty or more vehicles merit a new special recreational designation requiring complete environmental assessment and public hearings.

"They're just trying to price us out of existence," the off-road drivers said about the rumored hike in fees and changed classification.

Red Rock members appealed to their buddies on the county commission to designate their trails as county unimproved dirt roads, which would remove them from BLM jurisdiction. The commissioners complied by declaring the trails as Class D roads, but they didn't actually claim the right-of-ways.

But BLM's district director Gene Nodine raised legal barriers.

"They can go ahead and do that," he said. "But those are state regulations, and we have to deal with federal rules. We have never recognized Class D roads."

The county would have to obtain jurisdiction over the roads through the Federal Land Policy and Management Act, Nodine went on to explain. Then they could decide whether to charge users or not. And safety and environmental considerations would be on their shoulders.

Jim Stiles, editor of Moab's alternative newspaper, *The Zephyr*, interpreted the protests by jeepers as "symbolic of a greater, broader current of anger, distrust and frustration with government."

"Citizens feel impotent to bring any change or have any effect upon this huge bureaucracy that is supposed to serve us," he wrote. "None of us can even be sure who we should specifically be mad *at*. Is it the people at the local level who implement and enforce the rules and regulations? The people at the regional offices who write them? The people in Washington who tell the people in the regional offices [what] to write?"

In the case of the Jeep Safari, the protesters were again victorious. A number of discussions and an appeal to the Interior Bureau Land Appeals Board finally settled the affair in favor of the Red

Rock Four Wheelers. The tour would proceed, as usual, with minor alterations on some routes and limited numbers of vehicles on others.

But Canyonlands commercial tour operators still rankle about popular sightseeing routes being blockaded against traffic in the national parks. Backcountry guide Lin Ottinger's normally quiet voice reaches a high pitch when he rants about changes in Canyonlands.

"They claimed they weren't going to close any roads," he says, "but they closed over a hundred miles of roads. Probably two hundred of all the roads people used to go on. On the White Rim I moved lots of boulders they put in the road. They don't have the right to close the road! There's a hundred-foot corridor all the way around the White Rim, a hundred-foot-wide usage corridor. Down there now is an eight-foot road a mile long, less than an acre. Is that an adequate opportunity for the average person to see the parks? It isn't fair.

"The park, it says right on the bill, is for the benefit and use of the public. It's there to be used. It doesn't say to save it for some flabbledicking whapplebacker, or something that might be on the endangered list that no one ever saw before or since."

Canyonlands superintendent Harvey Wickware just shakes his head when discussing protected viewpoints such as the White Rim drive and Island in the Sky.

"I don't think we have destroyed the Island in the Sky District," he says. "There are those who think so. But that district is cleaner now, has less litter. We paved the road and built several overlooks with parking places that will accommodate touring buses and cars. The business of having vehicles going every which direction is crazy.

"The problem we have now is the mountain bike people going off the trail. There are some that think that it's a shame unless every hill that is trackless has their bicycle track going up one side and down the other."

Grand Teton National Park ran into trouble with the public, too. In 1990 the National Park Service announced its intention to rearrange existing traffic circulation patterns and facilities in the shadow of the famous peaks. Opposition came from all directions. Jackson Holers roared their disapproval of the proposed twenty-thousand-acre "Teton Corridor" between the village of Moose and Jenny Lake Lodge, ten miles to the north. Park visitors decried proposals to pave roads and "make coming to the Tetons like visiting the Washington Monument." The Jackson Hole Alliance for Responsible Planning rigorously opposed the plan to move park headquarters from Moose and construct a huge new visitors' center on a scenic bluff overlooking the famous elk refuge and interrupting the dramatic view of the Tetons. The historical society was appalled at the idea of replacing old buildings such as the Lucas homestead, Rockefeller attorney Harold Fabian's cabin, the famous Bar B C Dude Ranch, and Whitegrass Ranch with mobile home pads, modern houses, duplexes, and apartments for seasonal employees.

"The Fabian Ranch used to be Mrs. Lucas's ranch. She was the first woman to climb the Tetons and lived there alone for forty-five years," says society president Jack Huyler. "Why not restore some of these old cabins? Use *them* for their summer employees. Keep it in character."

While federal bureaucrats continue to evoke local wrath, typical regional rebelliousness is taking on a different dimension with the influx of new people and changing images of once-small communities. Instead of visiting all of their anger on the feds, locals now joust among themselves: rednecks versus tree-huggers, land speculators opposing no-growthers, those touting city beautification and stubborn defenders of rural funkiness. As the resort towns grow, their populations splinter, with concerned citizens alliances and special-interest groups organizing, meeting, petitioning, and even recalling elected officials.

Often the lines are drawn between newcomers and the old guard. And the distinction about who can impose upon whose rights becomes an issue that is difficult to resolve.

There is the question of private ownership and the right to do what one pleases with one's own property. Some residents whose families have lived on a plot of land for generations want to keep it as it is. Others desire to sell it and profit from the increased land values. They resent the greenhorns who barge in and call the shots.

Others, many of them recent in-migrants who are familiar with eroding environments from their former places of residence, feel strong emotions about preservation of the natural surroundings that attracted them. They respect personal property rights but also feel that decisions of land usage must consider the common welfare of the community.

In 1990, when there was a move for the town to annex about 840 acres of the Jackson Hole Hereford Ranch (formerly the Porter Ranch, homesteaded sixty years ago by executor Ralph Gill's father-in-law), local citizens were in an uproar. The property had presented an entry into town reminiscent of a Currier and Ives print, with rare wood-frame beaver-slide racks flipping hay into old-fashioned rounded stacks, grazing cattle, and a regal white frame farmhouse shaded by tall trees and bordered by rustic log cabins.

In winter, people were used to getting up early to watch Gill's ranch-hands drive horse-drawn hay sleds through the snowy fields to feed the stock. They liked the pungent smell of manure in the crisp air and watching steam rise from the nostrils of the animals rooting in the sweet alfalfa.

Jackson Hole preservationists dreaded losing another of the historic ranches that had given the town its character. Most of the livestock operations had been replaced by residential communities or resort developments. What worried the people more was that a few years before the Porter Trust had proposed building a Wal-Mart store on their South Park property. The project had been foiled only by public opposition in the county, whose residents wanted to retain their rural character. Now, with the possibility of his ranch annexing to the city, which had less stringent regulations than the county, Gill might construct high-density housing or a mobile home park on the scenic entryway into town.

"If it is indeed annexed, it's reasonable to suspect that the town will change the zoning from one unit per three acres to something that allows three or four homes on every acre. So that will create another little suburb," said Len Carlman, executive director of the Jackson Hole Alliance.

Concerned citizens wanted the town to adopt a comprehensive land-use plan before taking over the undeveloped property. When no action was taken, they accused the lame-duck mayor, Sam Clark, of negotiating an annexation agreement with Gill behind closed doors. They claimed he was "in Gill's pocket" and maintaining a "hurry-up attitude" in order to accomplish the task before leaving office.

Gill had endured a lot of static about the deal by the time I drove into the Porter Ranch and found him standing by the barn. I thanked him for agreeing to talk to me.

"I'm not sure I'm gonna," he said.

I followed him to a redwood picnic table in the back yard.

"Before we do any talking, I have one question," he said, straddling a bench. "Are you one of those environmentalists?"

"Aren't we all?" I replied.

"I suppose," he said, sitting down.

Gill, a former mayor who also served on the city council and county commission in the sixties and seventies, allowed that he didn't know what all the ruckus was about.

"I haven't sold anything," he said. But he protested that his family should be able to dispose of their holdings as they saw fit. They had paid taxes on the barren ground for sixty years, coaxed it into successful alfalfa production, and struggled with the fluctuating beef market.

"There's no future for ranching," he said. "There are only about five cow-calf operations left. My sons aren't interested in continuing the ranch. There's no incentive. They're moving or getting into electrical work, plumbing, etc."

Gill told me it was getting too expensive to drive cattle to the summer range with fewer fellow ranchers to share the work and costs, as they had traditionally done. Environmentalists were lobbying for the mountains to be "cattle-free by '93." Besides, existing subdivisions surrounded him on three sides and "the busiest highway in Wyoming" was on the other.

"You can't run cattle on an island," he said.

When challenged about selling out to a developer, Gill was adamant. "People who buy land have the right to do anything they want with it."

But Gill's annexation never happened.

Wyoming law mandates that a proposal for annexation must be publicly advertised thirty days prior to adoption, and at least two times. The city clerk duly delivered the information to the *Jackson Hole Guide*, but the newspaper inadvertently failed to publish the second notice. Attorney Larry Jorgenson, who was representing the city, learned about the legal failure in the process and advised the council that it would be unethical to proceed. The councilmen agreed with Jorgenson and the annexation matter was dropped.

"It's my belief they [council] would have pursued the annexation if not for the seemingly technical glitch," says Len Carlman.

The proposition went no further. With the subsequent election, Clark was out and the city council got some new blood and a different philosophy. There would be no annexations until some long-range master planning was accomplished, they ruled. And because any decisions affected everyone in the Hole, the newly elected officials took immediate steps to better the cooperation between city and county. Soon after taking office, they formed a Joint City-County Planning Board. The group meets every Monday to set common goals, policies, and regulations and to revise the thirteen-year-old land-use plan.

Moab's old sagebrush rebels got bounced off their county commission, too. In 1988 economic developers met environmentalists head on over construction of a toxic waste incinerator at Cisco, forty-five miles northeast of town. Reminiscent of the fracas over the nuclear waste dump near Canyonlands National Park in the early part of the decade, the emotional conflict became intense. Activists pulled up survey stakes at the proposed building site. The life of CoWest Incineration Corporation's president was even threatened via telephone.

Commissioners Ray Tibbetts and Jimmy Walker favored the project.

"My responsibility was to create situations for economic development," Walker says. "And that program there would have set up situations where we'd not only have a tax base but have monies paid into the county to help on services. It was this clean-air situation. It was going to put out these pollutants. They [the environmentalists] came on real strong with the Chicken Little philosophy."

Opponents gathered enough signatures to petition that the issue be placed on the general election ballot. That November, voters approved a referendum repealing zoning for incinerators.

"Because of our stand on that, that's how I got out of being a county commissioner," says Walker, somewhat bitterly.

Young upstarts are also affecting Moab's city council. A beautification drive is in force. Not everyone likes it. Tom Arnold is one of the dissenters.

"Tom Tom" is a self-proclaimed "character." The former "most popular professor in the College of Business" at Colorado State, Arnold holds master's degrees in economics and management, was a Navy flight instructor during World War II, and consulted for Massey-Ferguson Company. He is also curator of Tom Tom's Volkswagen Museum, the "world's most scenic V.W. yard." The town fathers call the collection of over two hundred "Bugs" "the disgrace."

Once you get through the door and past Spooky, the white-eyed watchdog at Arnold's warehouse, the dim light reveals a maze of tall metal stacks and random "artifacts" scattered on the floor. There is a musty smell of dust and dog. Atop Arnold's cluttered desk is a ceramic rendering of "the finger." A caricature of the gray-haired ex-professor with pipe and horn-rimmed glasses grins from the wall.

"I've been here seventeen years," he says proudly. "I'm in C-3 zoning. So about two years ago when they [city council] got on my case for having a junkyard, I said, 'I've got a museum and I'm the curator' "— and he offers an official museum business card as proof.

When county commissioner Merv Lawton spearheaded a regional cleanup campaign and noted that many of Arnold's neighbors had broken-down car chassis, old farm machines, mining equipment, or other pieces of debris on their grounds, he asked his friend to clean up his own place to set a good example.

"You may think it's trash," Arnold told him, "but I think it's beautiful."

Later Tom Tom learned the new beautification ordinance would not affect businesses. Mischievously, he gathered his neighbors together and had them each pay $10 for a business license.

"We'll make them artists," he said, "so we can say all these cars or whatever are sculptures."

Former councilman Dave Bierscheid contends that Arnold typifies many westerners. They don't want any ordinances. "We live in the West because we don't want to be organized. We want to have ten junk cars on our lot," he says.

"One man's junk is another man's gold," is an adage oft repeated in Moab. Main Street merchants hold the same philosophy regarding a proposed sign ordinance. People who have been in business for years take exception when some latecomer suddenly announces that their sign is too large, too high, not the right style or color.

"There are some people coming in now that want to change everything," says Moab Hardware dealer Don Knowles.

Particular resentment is leveled at newcomers from other resort towns, such as Park City, Telluride, and Aspen. Locals are suspicious of their motives and fearful that they plundered and ran from their former homes and will do the same to Moab.

Tom and Suzanne Shellenberger of Park City had been "southern Utah junkies" for over twelve years when they decided to move south. They came for the diverse environment—desert and mountain—and the fact that they could camp outdoors or cross-country ski all winter. In their view, they didn't *leave* Park City, they *adopted* Moab.

Tom, who had served on the ski resort city council, became the economic development director of Moab's chamber of commerce. He feels he has not been totally accepted by the community.

"You say you're from Park City, Aspen, or Telluride and it's almost like swearing to some people," he says. "But I don't think these people are working from a point of reality. Rather than working to get laws or ordinances on the books that will protect what's happening in town, they attack the people coming in: 'We don't want you to do what you did to Park City in our town.' Well, I moved to Moab because I like Moab the way it is. I didn't move here to make it a Park City."

Rather than fight the inevitable, some old-timers are content to let the new people do their will. Ralph Miller, who has weathered several booms and busts, claims he no longer has the drive or the clout needed to get involved. He's served on all of the committees, he has seen what has happened. "The miners have had to leave the area and as a result a lot of 'tree-huggers' or environmentalists have moved in," he says. "So now they're really becoming the driving force in politics. It's going to be a tough battle. You're seeing these changes taking place which are really kind of stirred up by these people that have seen these things happen in other communities."

Miller has come to the conclusion that he's better off selling the family's real estate and carrying the paper. "Play the role of the banker," he says. "That way it's not quite so demanding."

Miller sold the old Uranium Building that once housed his market and variety store. A Park City group restored the red-brick building into the Grand Emporium to sell art, mineral specimens, gifts, jewelry, and even yogurt.

As the face of Main Street metamorphoses in Moab and other towns and the population changes, there is a dichotomous philosophy about economic growth.

"There are as many factions here as you want to name,"

Shellenberger says. "There's the old miners; they want anything and everything. Anything would be okay with them as long as it provides jobs at $15 an hour.

"Then there's a group that doesn't want to see any changes. They like Moab the way it is, the funky, junky look of it.

"And then there's everybody else in between."

Often the conflicting forces of a community are organized into citizen action groups. According to Aspen city manager Carol O'Dowd, that town has activist organizations for protection of the environment, promotion of an art park and local theatre, a Hispanic task force, the Aspen-Pitkin County Housing Authority, and "a law firm that popped up for legal action."

"There's a coalition for everything in this town," she says. "In some ways I think Aspen is interesting because it's a microcosm of what's happening in cities throughout the country. We are seeing shifts from the pure representative type of government to participatory democracy, where your citizens are more actively involved and participating in the development of policy."

"The up side of all the groups is that you end up with a very active, involved citizenry," she adds. "You have citizens as well as council taking active leadership roles on various issues."

Activism isn't new to the West. Yet it doesn't operate like the torch-carrying lynch mobs of yesteryear that are depicted in old movies. Today's protagonists are equally passionate and idealistic. But instead of running headstrong on raw emotion, they are attempting to become schooled in the political process by attending and participating in city council meetings and community committee hearings.

When a flood of young adults hit Telluride in the early seventies, the local miners were more confused than convinced that tourism was the answer to their economic woes. Downtown's sleepy Colorado Avenue filled with long-haired out-of-staters who had master's degrees and doctorates but affected the appearance and shared the values of the unsettled sixties period. They lived in bunches in dilapidated old houses and supported themselves by the hand-to-mouth jobs of hammering nails, mixing drinks, and washing dishes—employment referred to as "Alpine Subsistence."

"At that time this town was still traditional," says Rick Silverman, who left the Bay area in 1972 to settle in the Colorado mountains. "It had been a hard-core mining town. We, as newcomers, would be described as hippies or counter-culturists. We were perceived as very threatening to those folks."

The threat became reality in a surprising way, however. In 1974, the youngsters decided the lackadaisical structuring of city government needed work. At that time there was little planning for the inevitable impacts of growth from tourism and development on the town's infrastructure—schools, police, sewers. Zoning was casual and the budding activists felt that the powerful new ski corporation appeared to be fighting against strengthening it.

Silverman and his buddies formed a coalition and took all the proper steps to run a slate of candidates for city council. To everyone's surprise, they succeeded in placing a new mayor and four councilmen in office. While all of the coalition's zoning battles were not won during their terms, the incentive for citizen participation took fire. A majority of the former activist hippies provides responsible leadership for the town today.

The Jackson Hole Alliance for Responsible Planning was initially formed in 1979 to safeguard the Teton County comprehensive land use plan. Implementation of the regulatory ruling passed two years before was threatened by the election of antagonistic candidates who gained a two-to-one majority on the county commission. Supporters of the plan feared the controls for which they had crusaded would be thrown in the trash.

Story Clark, wife of Snake Creek Ranch partner Bill Resor, rallied the troops. She enlisted the help of third-generation Jackson Holers Gene and Darrell Hoffman, Ted and Addie Donnan, Karl Wagner, and others as volunteers to monitor all of the commission meetings. The loyal few witnessed hours of deliberation before finally deciding that the issues were too complex, the meeting loads too heavy, and the time demands too intense for them to handle. They incorporated as the alliance and hired a paid director.

After twelve years, the alliance has grown to a membership of about eleven hundred dedicated to the protection of the natural environment and civic ambiance of Jackson Hole valley. Having witnessed its evolution from cowtown to tourist mecca, they fight everything from commercial strip development and denigration of open space to the demise of trumpeter swans.

A permanent, broad-based organization with a paid director and staff like the Jackson Hole Alliance is, unfortunately, an aberration. Most citizens' groups erupt and disband according to the dictates of the battle at hand. Leaders step forward, rally their cohorts, and make themselves known. They circulate petitions, speak up at hearings, force initiatives and referendums on the ballot—and then, after the outcome has been determined, they get on with their own lives.

With the question of growth foremost on the minds of western resort communities, most activist storms revolve around development. In Taos, New Mexico, a debate centers on airport expansion and construction of a $40-million residential and golf course project. Imperial Beach, California, dissenters are fighting high-rise condominiums on the beachfront. A group in Moab is concerned about a proposed performing arts amphitheater to be chiseled out of a redrock cliff above town. Park City's Community Coalition organized in 1990 in response to the city's sale of an abandoned schoolhouse, to be remodeled as a cultural center, along with adjacent publicly held open space, slated for construction of a multistory two-hundred-room hotel and conference center.

"I live in an area of Old Town," says Leslie Miller, coalition founder and president. "There's the old Carl Winter's School there with an adjacent four acres of property. In the Park City comprehensive master plan, that [four-acre] property was specifically referred to as open space and a potential park.

"So what took place almost a year ago was the city entered

negotiations with a developer from New York who proposed not only to renovate the old building but, in exchange for his renovation, to develop the additional acres that had been donated as open space."

Miller, who claims until that time she had been "a political couch potato," decided it was time to act. Her commitment was contagious. With other volunteers she collected approximately four hundred signatures on an informal petition requesting city council to delay a decision on the project until an urban design plan could be put in place.

"At that meeting, the city council took a vote and approved the proposal by the developer," Miller says. "We were pretty outraged by the way we were responded to and how our suggestion was treated. We felt that the city government was insensitive to the general public's interest in their own public land. So that was really the beginning of the Park City Community Coalition."

Citizens' action groups can make a difference. Miller's contingent succeeded in discouraging the New York developer to press plans for a hotel. Indeed, the coalition's outcry put a hold on the entire project. As a result of the reevaluation, there is a plan to turn the old school into a new city library and retain the open space as a park.

Frannie Huff, founder of Wyoming Woolens in Jackson Hole, had been too busy building up a business to pay much attention to local affairs. Within ten years her cottage industry that started with drink-can coolers made from fabric scraps had expanded into a sportswear manufacturing company with three retail stores, two factory outlets, and approximately fourteen hundred wholesale accounts throughout the country and abroad.

Then one day she read the "Street Talk" feature in the weekly newspaper. K-Mart and Wal-Mart were both looking for locations in Jackson. None of the five persons interviewed seemed to care one way or the other if such stores came into the area.

"I just couldn't believe it," Huff says. "Things had gone far enough. Next day I took out a quarter-page ad in the paper that said, 'No Wal-Mart. No K-Mart. Let's be smart. Help prevent this blight on

Jackson. Call Wyoming Woolens.' "

Huff followed up by attending council meetings, running more ads, and making personal telephone calls. Her campaign secured enough signatures on petitions and donations of money to successfully challenge the massive chains. Wal-Mart was barred from town. K-Mart, which succeeded in getting a special-use permit from outgoing mayor Clark, made concessions on size, design, signage, and landscaping.

While there is no doubt that citizen's action groups are counteracting growth impacts both on town character and the natural environment, Jackson's Len Carlman admits they cannot entirely stop what many persons deem progress.

"Most people who support the alliance point of view are basically against change," he says. "The moment people made that emotional connection to Jackson Hole in a certain condition, when that condition changed, that was a loss. So there's sort of gut-level, understandable, and reasonable resistance to change. I feel it myself.

"I am part of the change; I'm not a part of the old Jackson Hole. What I know about the old Jackson Hole is [the difference between] what we could see a number of years ago and what you can tell by looking at the landscape today. It would be incorrect for someone to think that they could come to our Jackson Hole and experience 'the last and best of the Old West.' We're not the last of the Old West. We're not even the Old West at all, so how could we be the best? We're really the best of the New West."

SiX: EAGLES ON THE HIGHWAY

There was no time to drape the patient. He was unconscious. Not responding to medication. Close to death. The blow had been so shattering that the heartbeat was weak and irregular. Dr. Paul Bingham, masked and gowned, bent beneath the glare of operating lights and reached for a scalpel. Deftly, he made an incision and thrust his hand into the chest cavity to massage the damaged heart. In a few moments he looked up at John and Marilyn Bicking, who were assisting him. He shook his head. The magnificent golden eagle was dead.

"There was another one just five days ago," Marilyn whispered. "It's got to stop."

It was about one-thirty on the morning of December 27, 1988, when the Bickings got back to their home in Moab. Dr. Bingham had called them late that afternoon. An Army staff sergeant had picked up the injured bird on Interstate 70, just out of Cisco. Returning to California after spending Christmas in Michigan, he drove sixty miles out of his way to deliver the eagle to the veterinary clinic in Spanish Valley. The scene had been repeated too frequently.

The Bickings had had it.

"I'm calling Miles," Marilyn said, picking up the phone.

Miles Moretti was the nongame manager of the county and regional wildlife resources division. Knowing the Bickings wouldn't be calling him in the middle of the night unless they were very upset, he listened sympathetically to their concerns.

John had all of the data on his computer. In the last two winters, vehicular collisions had wiped out thirty golden eagles and crippled eleven more. Twenty were killed in 1988 alone. The birds were hit while feeding on carrion or live prairie dogs and rabbits along the highway.

They were too big and slow to spread their six-foot span of wings and take flight quickly enough to escape speeding cars and trucks.

Most of the accidents occur on I-70 between Spotted Wolf and the Colorado state line, Marilyn told Moretti. The raptors use power poles as hunting perches. John had even pinpointed the danger area between mile posts 200 and 220. There must be some way to prevent the carnage.

Moretti promised to do what he could.

The Bickings started their personal letter-writing campaign next morning.

In the early 1980s, before the New York advertising executive and registered nurse moved from New Jersey to Moab, they had no idea that in a few years they would found and manage a volunteer raptor sanctuary. They purchased 280 acres five miles south and two miles east of town and looked into having their future home made into a wildlife preserve. But the conservation officer told them that what the area really needed was a raptor reserve.

"I said I'd love to do that," Marilyn says. "I went back to New Jersey and found a place to work for a couple of years to get experience with live raptors."

The Bickings returned to Utah in 1984 but have had no time to build their dream home. Instead, they live in town with a backyard full of Cooper's hawks, peregrine falcons, kestrels, prairie falcons, eagles, and Cyclops, a one-eyed great horned owl.

Taking out one week each month to commute to his New York office, John joins Marilyn in the care, release, and round-the-clock rescue missions of injured or orphaned raptors. Their crusade, triggered by distress over that golden eagle slaughtered on the freeway in 1988, convinced Utah Power & Light Company to modify strategic power poles with metallic triangles to eliminate perching posts. And the Utah Department of Transportation planted the world's only six signs that warn: Eagles On Highway. The preventive measures helped. Today more eagles are surviving the flat, straight desert speedway.

Perhaps we could view the golden eagles on the highway as a kind of metaphor for the endangered rural towns of the West. Just as we cannot completely stop speeding traffic on the interstate freeway, we cannot slam the brakes on growth in successful resort communities. But care and thought similar to that of the Bickings for the eagles might enable the small towns of western America to salvage their particular essence.

"I'm convinced that the places that retain their character and identity are going to be enormously successful in the future because there's going to be so few of them," says Terrell J. Minger, president of Robert Redford's Institute for Resource Management in Denver, Colorado.

Rural areas that have been "discovered" as resorts have singular qualities that warrant protection: authentic Victorian houses; rustic pinewood Main Streets; sculptured natural ridgelines on surrounding hills; pastures with cattle grazing around haystacks; mountain meadows filled with wildflowers and game; mysterious deserts; inviting waterways; and a diverse population that takes time to be "neighbors."

If we're not careful, these small towns will all become imitation Swiss Alpine villages or sprawling Anywhere, U.S.A. The trouble is that we're tardy about recognizing the threat. We're sitting at the table gorging on "all the shrimp you can eat for $7.99." We don't think about the consequences of eating too much—or running out of shrimp.

It's a classic problem. We did the same thing with historic buildings and sites. After World War II, we were on a "modernistic" binge. Old was out. We allowed the wrecking ball to destroy many of our treasures before we recognized the fact that they were our heritage.

We showed the same disregard for the environment. The woods. Sparkling streams. Clean air. Open space. We thought it was all unending until we forced the reality of irreparable loss one time too many.

"The reason most of these places get in trouble is they know intuitively something is wrong, not quite right, a little out of control, but don't really understand it," Minger says.

He compares the situation to the boiling frog syndrome. Drop the frog in a cauldron of boiling water and it will have the sense to jump out. Put it in a pan of cool water and gradually increase the temperature by increments, and it will boil to death.

Or like the eagle. He doesn't hear the approaching truck, and by the time he sees it, it's too late to fly.

"My sense is that in all these communities—Santa Fe, Vail, Park City, Jackson—the ultimate point where the quality of life reversed and got out of balance came very subtly and incrementally and the public didn't comprehend it as quickly as they should have," says Minger.

"Each year, even if you're growing at three-and-a-half percent, eventually the compounding of that growth gets you in trouble. They don't seem to understand that these resorts have life cycles. A building time. A stabilizing time. Then a time maybe when you need to be renewing but you don't have to be growing any more. Let the growth go somewhere else. Don't try to capture it all."

Fortunately, a new awareness is coming. It even reached the pages of *The New Yorker* in a Frank Modell cartoon depicting a couple picnicking under a lone tree on a bucolic hillside. Broad vistas of meadows spread below them.

"It's so lovely out here you wonder why they have it so far from the city," the woman says.

The trick is keeping the city away from that bucolic hillside, which is no easy task. Resorts are as individualistic as people. Each possesses its own history, a unique physical setting, a distinctive personality. The pernicious homogenization that threatens to clone them into oblivion occurs in different stages. While the Jacksons, Aspens, and Santa Fes attempt to shift gears into reverse and remedy past mistakes, the Moabs are only now coping with the first wave of post-1970s development. And their optimistic anticipation of the future is tempered by the dread of "becoming another Park City or Telluride."

August St. John, professor of marketing and future studies at

Long Island University in New York, sees the development of American resorts as a five-stage life cycle: welcome; development; resentment; confrontation; destruction.

"By 'destruction,'" author Andrew Nemethy explains, "St. John doesn't mean a physical catastrophe, but the ruin or disappearance, as growth overwhelms a resort area, of the things that were the original attractions: neighborliness and sense of community, a rural landscape, small-town atmosphere, friendliness, low traffic, and low taxes."

Perhaps St. John's contention that the destruction period is inevitable can be mitigated by a heightened awareness that these resorts are little jewels and deserve exceptional care.

"The people that live in these small communities are trustees of these places, more than in a normal big city," Minger says. "They have special responsibilities to the environment, to the point that they don't get overdeveloped and become U.S.A. Everywhere."

There are a number of philosophies on how to manage such trusteeship. Some people would choose to bar the door and maintain the status quo. Others speak of engineering a "controlled growth." And another sector, usually those whose economy is on the skids, flings the gate wide open. Each of these approaches is fraught with pluses and minuses.

"No-growthers" contend that a community should not be forced to outrun its natural resources or face deterioration of lifestyle through overcrowding. They realize that they cannot really shut everyone out, but they do the best they can by imposing caps—absolute upper limits—on residential developments. These quotas automatically limit in-migration and population growth. Often, champions of this philosophy are those comfortably ensconced as newcomers who want to keep their recent discovery to themselves.

"Everybody always says we wish the door had been closed just after we got here," Jacksonite John Huyler says.

"But darn it all, as Doc Gray said, 'A bucket gets full.' When is this valley full? I think it's full now. I think bigger isn't better and they can have this town grow, grow, grow and more businesses will bust, bust, bust. Why not keep the quality thing we've got, encourage tourism, discourage lots of people coming in and settling? Discourage the big money coming in because prices keep going out of sight."

In 1975, Aspen imposed a growth cap. According to former mayor Bill Stirling, the move was meant "to cool the heels of the real estate developers' feeding frenzy, but it also helped us preserve our egalitarian society."

But Carol O'Dowd, Aspen's city manager, contends the closed-door policy caused problems.

"The community here said we want no growth so we're going to slap on all these controls," she says. "Well, they didn't look through to the future. If you make a commodity that restrictive, what happens? It's been proven in this country since we began: the price goes up. It becomes a hot product. And that's what happened to Aspen. Pitkin County said we're going to make it so expensive to develop that people won't come in. What they forgot is that there are people in this world to whom 'so expensive' is very attractive."

Proponents of "controlled growth" contend that posting No Trespassing signs is unrealistic. It only serves to escalate the price of real estate and discriminate against the young, the poor, the old, and minorities. It encourages urban sprawl and air pollution from an overload of service employees forced to commute long distances.

"Very few people say they don't want change," says Park City public affairs director Myles Rademan. "Most people are saying, how can we control our change, manage it?"

Instead of turning their backs on in-migration altogether, these people are looking for "clean industry" to add diversity to the tourist-oriented economy. At the same time, they want to retain the small-town lifestyle they hold so dear. In order to accomplish both goals, many communities have adopted a system of allocations to induce a phased, slower growth mode.

Boulder County, Colorado, a valley comprised of ten municipalities, is often held up as a model for population management. During the 1970s, the county's largest town, Boulder, experienced a growth surge of almost eighty percent. In 1977, the Boulder Valley comprehensive plan was drawn to limit new dwelling units to 450 per year for five years. In a competitive program offering a given number of building permits designed to hold population expansion to two percent, projects built in the city core or those providing moderate-priced, energy-efficient homes were favored. On a hundred-point grading system, twenty points were awarded for affordable housing units.

Since 1982, the quota has been modified several times, but growth has been contained to two percent or under. In one decade, the county's growth fell from forty-four percent to approximately twelve percent.

Minger, a former assistant city manager in Boulder, admits there are always some tradeoffs when restrictive blueprints for a town are made, but sometimes the things you give up are still better than destroying the place altogether.

"A whole bunch of developers went away," he says. "A little bit of the bargain in all of this was that the cost of real estate still went up. It didn't go up crazily, but [it still went up] steadily. It caused certain people not to be able to afford to live in the city. But [finally] they got federal monies to build senior citizen and moderate housing."

A Park City attorney, Tom Clyde, isn't so sure the tradeoffs are worth the sacrifices. In 1991, he joined a group of other civic leaders on a city-sponsored junket to study city-county relationships in Boulder and Fort Collins, Colorado. He found the automobile traffic in the "model town" of Boulder "insufferable."

"They put this regulation on residential growth and rave about how wonderful that was, but they didn't put any regulation on commercial growth. So after this went into place, they went out and got IBM with eight thousand jobs and some other big employers. Huge,

huge campuses of high-tech industry with enormous employment. What you get is people commuting from Denver to Boulder to work.

"My car was burglarized while I was there listening to the mayor tell us there was no crime in Boulder. The cop that investigated it lived in Denver, as did everybody else who worked on the police force because they can't afford to live in Boulder.

"The planner in Boulder lives in Fort Collins and commutes; the Fort Collins planner lived in Boulder and made the commute the other way. They're trying so hard to maintain an individuality between those two cities but the reality is that each one is a suburb of the other and the traffic back and forth was like rush hour all the time."

Clyde and his fellow travelers returned home fearing the same scenario was threatening Park City.

According to economist Thayne Robson, the situation isn't all that unique.

"I don't know any place that has been able to effectively impose a controlled growth policy," he says. "There will always be a real estate or resort venture that is betting on and promoting future growth. Bringing the myriad of business enterprises into the community to try to get a mix that would be consistent with the controlled-growth policy is something that I think no community I know of has ever been able to do. Towns are either too successful or they're not successful enough. If you can find one anywhere in the West that you think is just right, please call it to my attention."

Jimmy Walker, of Moab, has seen his county in heyday and bust situations a couple of times. He prefers the former. "The best thing this country has in selling itself is its beauty," he says. "The northern part of our county has large oil, gas, and tar sands [deposits] that might create an economic movement that would offset the loss here. One of the best things we have in Grand County is the diversity, the economic potential. What we could do economically if people would get some of these cobwebs out of their heads! Grand County could have the best of two worlds."

"I don't think our town can really absorb lots and lots," counters

Moab environmentalist Ken Sleight. "Some people think we ought to get as many people as we can and we'll think about overdevelopment later. We're so weak that people come along to the commissioners with proposals and we'll take anything. We'll take the incinerator. We're sitting ducks to the developers. Anybody that comes in and says we've got a $3 or $4 million-dollar project, we'll take it, whether it's detrimental or not."

Debates on how to handle the inevitable changes have broadened during the past twenty years since the onset of what many people refer to as the "quiet revolution." In the early 1970s, in the wake of a flurry of popular initiatives, the federal government and states became increasingly involved in problems of environmental degradation, population management, open space, traffic congestion, urban sprawl, and so on. Today, approximately half of the states mandate that local governments adopt a comprehensive plan addressing these questions. In other states, the planning process is often undertaken by regional administrations or local city halls.

It would seem that the resort communities we are discussing have a planning advantage over big cities and metropolises. Despite the rapid changes they are undergoing, they are still essentially small towns, with a contained geography and a permanent residency that is reachable. Rather than advocacy of the "pro-growth," "no-growth," or "controlled-growth" policies, the development of a special "customized-growth" philosophy might be more appropriate.

Customized growth takes into account a community's pride in the uniqueness of its landscape and mixture of people. Rather than acceptance of a rote, generalized comprehensive master plan for the future, citizens affix their own stamp to a pattern that will produce continued stimulation of the economy and sustenance of a desired lifestyle.

"Every town has to chart its own destiny," says Aspen's former mayor Stirling. "I know we've missed some things and it's hell playing catch-up."

We are sipping hyacinth spice tea in the upstairs coffeehouse of the Explore Bookshop on Main Street in Aspen. Browsers ruffle through volumes on shelves dominating the restored Victorian house. Symphonic music plays. The famous Aspen glitz is absent. A thoughtful Stirling offers some advice to Moab and other burgeoning resorts who speak of avoiding "Aspenization." He suggests original master planning.

"What a comprehensive master plan does is give a community a chance to chart the destiny of a town in the image they would like it to be as opposed to an image that somebody brings from the outside. If you don't set some standards, invariably those outsiders who discover these towns and have money will insinuate themselves into the town and imprint their own view of what they think it ought to be."

The first step in achieving this goal is getting people together to talk. A refreshing sense of reason about the necessity of communication is beginning to surface in many western regions. City and county planners, councilmen, developers, activists, and citizens who are just plain confused are deciding it's time to put their heads together and seek creative solutions to the problems of growth.

Public affairs director Myles Rademan organized Community Vision '89 after *Snow Country Magazine* rated Park City and Summit County "as the most super-dynamic area in the country between 1978 and 1987." In over forty informal living-room coffee klatches, four hundred town residents expressed their views about "who we are" and "what we want." A few months later, a similar two-day planning workshop included a number of groups from the county, as well. Not surprisingly, they wanted it all: open space, recreational facilities, quality schools, affordable housing, more and better shopping, no traffic congestion, economic opportunities, and clean air.

The following year, a Successful Communities Workshop picked the brains of over three hundred Jackson Holers. What did *they* want? Open space, recreational facilities, quality schools, affordable housing, more and better shopping, no traffic congestion, economic opportunities, clean air.

The underlying purpose of these and other citizen meetings is to create a vision for the future. They provide all factions of a community or region an opportunity to express themselves. The anticipated end result is a viable master plan whose regulations have been devised with consideration of the issues most important to area residents and of the goals they have agreed on.

I favor regionalizing this approach to customized growth. As the resort towns achieve more and more success, the impacts spread further into the surrounding counties. Rather than seeking independent identities and harboring fractious "hick farmer versus city slicker" attitudes, adjoining cities and counties should coauthor a master plan.

Sometimes city and county commissioners favor a moratorium to suspend development while the master planning is in progress. Such "interim regulation" is a controversial process. Builders and real estate developers oppose moratoriums and claim tightening the market only serves to skyrocket housing costs. City fathers argue they need time to make a critical analysis and formulate solutions.

"We did a couple of moratoriums when I was in Vail," says Minger. "I think there's no question that, [if] you put the lid on, when you take it off it's like a pressure cooker. However, if you really take time during the moratorium, get yourself organized, and do the kind of work that needs to be done, I think a moratorium may be helpful."

In 1991, Jackson Hole residents were at odds about a proposed moratorium on development of environmentally sensitive lands. Teton County commissioners, still "hot" after the fracas over the town's possible annexation of the Porter Ranch, wanted time to work with the city on a new land-use plan. They feared riparian lands and other special parcels might be developed before revisions to the code could be finished.

After much sometimes-bitter debate, they compromised on a more stringent eighteen-month restriction on construction. The adopted plan targeted a one-year halt on all commercial planned unit developments, new subdivisions bordering riverbanks, streams, or the state highway and on ridgelines or hillsides with a twenty-percent slope. Regulations encouraged clustering of homes to preserve open space and protect wildlife habitats and exempted individual building permits or previously approved plats or variances.

When Sedona, Arizona, gained incorporation, the first matter of business was formulating a master plan. And top priority of that project was preservation of open space. In Sedona, as in Jackson, Moab, and many other resort towns, a majority of the surrounding country is owned by the U.S. Park Service, Forest Service, BLM, or some other federal or state agency. Sometimes up to eighty-five percent of the land is government property. This establishes premium value for remaining privately owned acreage.

Naturally, the highest and best use for land adjacent to resorts is for condominium complexes, residential communities, or shopping centers. Developers are clamoring for these prize parcels and are willing to pay exorbitant prices for them. But the community wants to retain the broad vistas and natural beauty that make the area so special. The problem is how to accomplish this when the individual property ownership—and the right to dispose of one's property as one sees fit—is regarded as sacrosanct.

"There's no way in a free society where you rely on private property institutions that you can prevent growth, unless you want to get all the land into public ownership," says Thayne Robson. "And even that's difficult. In my view, communities who want to preserve must be willing to pay the price of that preservation. They've got to ante up and do it."

Boulder, Colorado, is lauded as an exemplary city for doing just that. In 1959, voters passed a referendum to establish a "blue line" bordering the scenic Flatiron Mountains west of town. The imaginary line lay one hundred feet below the reservoir's mean water level where city water service terminated. Automatically, construction of houses climbing the hillsides or sitting atop ridgelines was precluded by restrictions on pumping water uphill.

Five years later, in reaction to a proposed 155-acre resort targeted for the cherished foothills, the city purchased the Enchanted

Mesa as open space. In another three years, citizens approved a one-percent city sales tax, with forty percent earmarked for a greenbelt around the perimeter of town. Subsequent bonds backed by sales tax revenues have continued these programs. Much of the city-owned-and-managed open space is leased out for ranching and farming. Other areas remain as tallgrass prairies, wetlands, mountain slopes, and forest.

Physical expansion was also addressed. The city and county collaborated on a joint Boulder Valley comprehensive plan to guide development, control urban sprawl, and protect open space. They mandated a limit on building permits to hold annual population growth to two percent. A development excise tax paid for new developments to buy into the existing infrastructure. The regional shopping area was renewed and expanded and outlying malls were resisted. A transportation management system was put in place. Historic districts were renovated, building height limitations implemented, and bike and pedestrian trails extended.

Story Clark, founding organizer of the Jackson Hole Alliance for Responsible Planning, followed a different path to preserving open space in her valley. About the same time she helped form the alliance, she and Romaine Jean Hocker received a grant from the Isaac Walton League of America to collaborate on a study entitled "Quick Eyes on Private Land." Their research revealed that many people are willing to take voluntary action to guarantee that their private land will be protected in the future. Consequently, Clark established the Jackson Hole Land Trust.

Land trusts have been in existence since the mid-nineteenth century and are regaining popularity as tools for environmental and community preservation. "Different land trusts may save different types of land for different reasons," Hocker said at a meeting in Estes Park, Colorado. "Some preserve farmland to maintain economic opportunities for local farmers. Some preserve wildlife habitat to ensure the existence of an endangered species. Some protect land in watersheds to improve or maintain water quality...the reasons for protecting land are as diverse as the landscape itself."

Clark's group began preserving open space and view corridors by getting conservation easements from Earl Hardeman, Paul Walton, and other local ranchers. With the spiraling price of land and the insatiable appetite of speculators, the cattlemen, mostly seniors, were becoming concerned about their estate planning. Their wealth was in the land. If they didn't dispose of it before their death, their families might have to sell out at sacrificial prices to pay inheritance taxes on the inflated value of the property. If they sold or gave tax-free easements that forfeited development rights on their property in perpetuity, they could retain use and ownership of their land and reap tax benefits as well. And Teton County would wind up with one less subdivision or shopping mall.

"When they die, fifty-five percent of the determined value of their estate must be paid in cash to the federal government," Clark says. "This is very regressive for the ranchers and farmers because they have all their worth tied up in their land. Inheritance tax will put the rancher out of business."

Hardeman, a former rodeo commentator with a suntan to the top of his balding head, has been a stockman all of his life. Filmed for a British Broadcasting System video series as a typical American rancher, the sixty-five-year-old cowboy is now retired. When failing health made it difficult for him to saddle his own horse, he decided it was time to sell the cattle and transfer a portion of his share of the family ranch to the Jackson Hole Land Trust.

"Hell, I can make twice as much money after paying the income tax," he says. "It takes ten head of cows to make the interest to make a profit at the end of the year. It just don't make sense. So my feeling is to sell some of it and walk on some of it."

Paul Walton put his entire two-thousand-acre ranch into the trust. For years to come travelers on the Wilson Road will enjoy scenes of his cattle grazing in the hayfields with a backdrop of the Teton Range.

Not all cattlemen are in the position to do this, however.

"Some of the land will be dedicated," says former governor and U.S. senator Cliff Hansen, "but for ranchers that have no other assets than the land itself it's unrealistic in my mind to expect them to dedicate land to open space. Rather, they would subscribe to the belief that if it's important to other people, let them buy it and then keep it as much open space as they choose."

As the number of landowners who are able and willing financially to give the development rights away has been almost exhausted, the Jackson Hole Land Trust is doing just that.

"Now we're having to get more aggressive and find individuals who can afford to buy land, protect it, and lease it back to the rancher," says Clark.

The trust also raises funds to purchase acreage itself. In 1989, the group took over the Wilson village square for an old-fashioned carnival to cap a three-month fundraising campaign. Kids ran sack races, rodeoed on stick horses, competed at painting horseshoes, and played games while adults bid on auction items and partied in western barbecue style. With contributions ranging from one dollar to one thousand (and a half-million-dollar ante from the county), the trust succeeded in raising almost $2 million dollars. They used the money to buy a large ranch on the outskirts of Wilson.

One of the greatest land conservation coups was finalized in November 1991. For an undisclosed amount exceeding $4 million dollars, the Jackson Hole Land Trust bought the 760-acre Hatchet Ranch in the Buffalo Valley preservation area on the eastern entry corridor into the Hole. The trust then sold 680 acres to Dick and Barbara Carlsberg, with a conservation easement limiting construction on the parcel to a single private home. Then the U.S. Forest Service purchased the remaining 180 acres and conservation easement from the trust for $2.8 million.

"It's a beautiful piece of property," said land trust executive director Day Breitag. "It's the first thing you see as you come over (Togwotee) Pass."

The influence of private citizens in preventing runaway

development from overtaking their community should not be understated. In addition to forming groups such as land trusts and the alliance, they should resist being lulled into a sense of security by the knowledge that a master plan is in place. A master plan should be reviewed and revised every five or ten years. But often, by the time many communities get around to studying old plans or authoring new ones, there are already developments that are grandfathered into the picture and promoters are pushing hard for additional pet projects. On top of this, those who own acreage of scarce, undeveloped land want, and can get, top dollar. When people don't pay attention, the bulldozers descend seemingly unannounced.

The majority of residents in Summit County, Utah, paid scant attention to a master plan until a feud erupted over the proposal of two shopping centers on the entryway to Park City, consisting of a K-Mart on one side of Kimball's Junction and a Wal-Mart and a factory outlet on the other. As if this were not enough, a massive expansion of Park West Ski Area and a number of large residential subdivisions in the Snyderville meadows were also on the drawing boards. Conceivably, commercial and residential sprawl would snake all the way from Parley's Summit—halfway to Salt Lake City—to Old Town Park City.

Concerned citizens attending a town meeting called by the local KPCW community radio station on May 23, 1991, were jolted by a report from Lee Nellis. Hired as a consultant to revamp the Snyderville Basin development code, written in 1982, Nellis told the stunned group that the original plan "was submitted for the fancy price of $2,600 as a project done by six of my students." Nellis further stated that, despite the fact that people have since suggested transportation and open space acquisition plans, neither has materialized. "That's the plan you've been using," he said. "There was never any attention [after] 1982…the process stopped with what was submitted."

It was while she was hiking on the Knolls north of Mammoth Lakes, California, that commissioner Mercedes Talley realized that her town's general plan needed review. Looking down on the Shady Rest parcel that was being proposed for affordable housing, and on the Bluffs, where a residential development was being considered, Talley was horrified. Maps and studies presented to the commission made sense on paper. But her panoramic view of town brought home the "real world." There were other big promotions on the table with names like Lodestar and North Village, as well as an expansion to Snowcreek. She wondered about things like density, greenbelts, architecture, color, and commercial space. She decided these projects needed more thought.

Talley rallied her fellow commissioners, the planning staff, a state forester, the Mono County supervisor, and a couple of citizens and reporters. They went to the top of Mammoth Mountain and toured Panorama Dome and the Knolls ski trail. They returned with renewed conviction to update the master plan. "We can't go back and change things that were approved before the town even came into existence," said commission chairwoman Helen Thompson. "The challenge now is to make the best of what's left."

Making the best of what's left can be a sad prospect. But it's a fact of life in our disappearing rural and mountain West. More than ever we must consider our actions. Irreversibility is a reality often recognized too late.

The Silver King Coalition Mines tramway terminal was the pride of Park City and a wonder of the western mining world. One man could operate cables with huge buckets that hauled tons of coal up to the mine works and delivered raw ore back to waiting railroad cars. Even after the mines closed, the tall, barn-red, turn-of-the-century building intrigued artists and photographers and its image was used as the ski corporation's logo until 1982, when vandals torched the frame structure, burning it to the ground.

In 1989, developers announced plans for the site where the Coalition building once stood, along with the restored Union Pacific depot, Rio Grande office, and old-time Utah Coal and Lumber building. When citizens learned about the Vail-style $60 million-dollar commercial/residential complex to cover approximately five hundred thousand square feet and include some structures seven stories high, there was strong negative reaction.

Finally, after many public hearings and renegotiations with the city, a compromise was struck. Developers, persuaded to "make the best of what is left," agreed to reduce the project by one hundred thousand square feet and limit heights to four stories. A projected extension of ski runs to the Town Lift, which would close a main thoroughfare into Old Town, was tabled for further discussion.

But we must constantly be aware of what is going on in our communities. As the Redford Institute's Terrell Minger warns, paraphrasing Thomas Jefferson's words, "The price of a good community is eternal vigilance. You get the master plan and you think it's done. But it isn't done. It's a living document. The community is changing every day and somebody has to be paying attention all the time."

NOTES

ON THE CUSP OF CHANGE

p. 27 "The population had risen…" *The Moab Story* (brochure).

p. 29 "Americans in general…in pristine wilderness." Ward Roylance, *Enchanted Wilderness Association Bulletin*, no. 2 (August 1971).

p. 41 "People kept coming in…find agates." James Armstrong, "The Dinosaur Man," *Ford Times*, April 1984.

p. 41 "There were arches…pot of gold." Ron Thoreson, "Canyonlands Birthday," *Canyon Country Visitors' Guide*, Summer 1989.

p. 44 "Before construction…dirt roads." Ward Roylance, "The Incredible Desecration of Dead Horse Point," *Enchanted Wilderness Association Bulletin*, no. 2, (August 1971).

p. 44 "…use the influence…this situation." Letter from Ward Roylance to Governor Calvin L. Rampton, November 4, 1971.

p. 45 "The uranium industry is sick…" Karen M. Mangeson, "Moab Seeks More Tourism and N-Waste Repository," *Deseret News*, September 7, 1983.

p. 46 "It was a battle…community identity." Ken Sleight, "Oh Moab, Whither Thou Goest…," *Catalyst*, April–May 1990.

PLACE OF EMPOWERMENT

p. 65 "Sedona is a dead-end…happen there," Kate Ruland-Thorne, *Experience Sedona Legends and Legacies*, Thorne Enterprises, 1989.

p. 67 "Sedona was becoming…you name it." Ibid.

HOW THE WILD WEST WAS LOST

p. 89 "A dude is one…sitting down." Virginia Huidekoper, *The Early Days in Jackson Hole*, Grand Teton Natural

History Association, 1978.

p. 89 "Top of the line...strictly adhered to." *Dude Ranches Out West*, Union Pacific Railroad Co. promotional pamphlet.

p. 89 "...a ranch owner...rolled into one." Struthers Burt, *Diary of a Dude-Wrangler*, Charles Scribner's Sons, 1938.

p. 91 "Whatever the facts...their problems." Robert W. Righter, "Another Way—Enter the National Park Service," *Crucible for Conservation: The Struggle for Grand Teton National Park*, Colorado Associated University Press, 1982.

LITTLE TOWN BLUES

p. 108 "In a 1990...real estate developers." Jim Danneskiold, "Santa Fe Losing Its Charm for Residents, Poll Shows," *Albuquerque Journal*, February 21, 1990.

p. 111 "wealthy outsider...people out." Camille Flores, "Saint or Sinner," *Santa Fe Sun*, March 1991.

p. 112 "The New Agers...our culture." Russell Chandler, "Bad Vibes Rock Arizona's New Age Mecca," *Los Angeles Times*, *Salt Lake Tribune*, August 25, 1991.

p. 115 "The locals explained...Ridgway area." "Worried Ridgway Residents Voice Development Concerns," Art Goodtimes, *The Telluride Times-Journal*, October 4, 1990.

p. 118 "...a clerical nightmare." Madeleine Osberger, "Apts are available...for big bucks," *Aspen Times*, October 4, 1990.

p. 119 "... scared that the town...quiet and lifeless." John Bowermaster, "Aspen: The Call of the Wild," *New York Times Magazine*, January 21, 1990.

p. 119 "...to maintain Aspen's...full-time." John Colson, "Land Costs May Be Gift from City," Aspen Times, September 20, 1990.

p. 129 "... bigger than Vail..." Richard L. Fetter and Suzanne Fetter, *Telluride from Pick to Powder*, Caxton Printers, 1979.

FIGHTING WORDS

p. 138 "We are convinced...in the future." "Grand County Lists Reasons for Opposing BLM wilderness," *Times-Independent*, July 5, 1979.

p. 138-39 "We fear that many...lives here." Ibid.

p. 90 "Gene Day was...constitutional rights." Raymond Wheeler, "Boom! Boom! Boom! War on the Colorado Plateau," *Reopening the Western Frontier.*"

p. 140 "It was just a matter..." Ibid.

p. 141 "They can go ahead...Class D roads." Ken Davey, "Big Fee Increase Aimed at Killing Safari, Group Says," *Times-Independent*, August 16, 1990.

p. 141 "Citizens feel impotent...to write?" Jim Stiles, "The Jeep Safari vs. The BLM," *The Zephyr*, September, 1990.

EAGLES ON THE HIGHWAY

p. 158 "It even reached..." Cartoon, Frank Modell, *The New Yorker*, July 23, 1990.

p. 159 "By 'destruction'...low taxes." Andrew Nemethy, "Resorts Go Up...and Down," *Snow Country*, November 1990.

p. 167-68 "Different land trusts...landscape itself." Chris Elfring, "Preserving Land through Local Land Trusts," *The Land Trust Alliance*, February 1989.

p. 169 "It's a beautiful...(Toqwottee) Pass." *Jackson Hole Guide*, From The Park Record, November 1991.

p. 171 "We can't go back...into existence." Jeff Putman, "Planners View Mammoth from a Different Angle," *The Review-Herald*, August 5, 1990.

Raye C. Ringholz

K. C. Muscolino